WHITLEY —

WITH INFINITE
LOVE + GRATITUDE
FOR YOUR WORK,

Bobby B.

PAST LIFE
JOURNEYING

EXPLORING PAST, BETWEEN, and FUTURE LIVES

R.C. BARANOWSKI

Edited by Brenda Dammann

http://www.creativeinc.net

Paperback ISBN: 978-1-66789-789-9
eBook ISBN: 978-1-66789-790-5

Illustration and cover design by Red Pill Junkie,
absurdbydesign.com
Author photo by Randi Janelle

With infinite love and gratitude to William
and Diane Swygard for their innovation
of the Awareness Techniques,

to Paul Newell and Miguel Parades for
guiding me on my first Past life journey,

and to all the brave participants in the Past Lives Project.

TABLE OF CONTENTS

Author's Note   1

Introduction   3

Part 1: Discovering the Awareness Technique   11

- My Origin Story   12
- From Skeptic to Enthusiast   15
- The Awareness Technique   19
- *Running* a Past Life   30
- *Running* Tip: Costumes   33
- Dying and the Non-Physical Experience Between Lives   37
- *Running* Tip: Names as Placeholders   45

Part 2: The Heart of the Matter   47

- Other Practitioners Working without Hypnosis: Morris Netherton & Roger Woolger   48
- Guiding Group Past Life Journeys   52
- Dick Sutphen and Shadow Work: Both Victim and Perpetrator   57
- Healing with the Release Technique and Ho'oponopono   64
- Shamanic Journeys and Psychonauts   68
- *Running* Tip: Discernment   75

Part 3: It's About Time!   77

- Dr. Bruce Goldberg: Non-Linear Time, Simultaneous and Future Lives   78
- Michael Talbot: Past Lives and Time in a Holographic Universe   86

- Eric Wargo on Time Loops and the Block Universe Theory   95
- George—My 29th Century Future Life   102

Part 4: Past Life Journeying in Action   107

- "I Think I'm Just Making this Up"   108
- Past Life Journeying as a Spiritual Practice   116
- Instructions for Guiding a Past Life Journey   120
- *Running* tip: *Running* Past Lives by Yourself   126
- My Solo Session Process   132
- Postscript   136

End Notes   138

AUTHOR'S NOTE

I once attended a UFO conference where one of the presenters used the following quote as the first slide in their PowerPoint deck:

> *All of the material in this presentation has been channeled. Deal with it.*

This produced a nervous chuckle from the crowd, but the presenter made their point and, I assume, established their credentials for that specific audience.

This inspired me to declare the following:

> *None of the material in this book from my personal Past, Between, and Future lives has been channeled. Just go with it.*

Apart from my research, all the material in *Past Life Journeying* has been obtained by me, personally, through the use of the question-and-answer technique inspired by William and Diane Swygard's book *Awareness Techniques*. I adapted my own variation of their process over several decades through the accumulation of my own personal work, hundreds of one-on-one sessions with clients from all over the world, plus my work with both online and in-person groups. I would not have the needed confidence to present this material—and self-publish it at my own expense—if I were channeling it from a non-physical collaborator or post-material personality. (Although post-physical consciousness and "discarnate entities" *do* factor into my odyssey, as you'll see later.)

My sources are my own Past and Future selves; it is their "database" of experience to which I connect, along with my awareness of their internal thoughts and emotional processes, both personal and universal. I perceive this to be different—and perhaps more authoritative—than receiving channeled information from an external "database," which may have never incarnated in human form. Yes, I expect to get some pushback from channelers when they read this, but my conclusions are the result of decades of intense and often challenging inner journeying.

I continue to be amazed by the power and simplicity of the Awareness Technique. To make this door-opening experience available to anyone interested in pursuing it on their own, I have included my own version of the original instructions which have evolved and expanded over hundreds of my own and my clients' sessions. But while I base my Past Life Journeying practice on Swygard's original text, I find the original technique very cerebral in accessing information that comes from the Past life experience.

My innovation—if I can call it that—is to move the experience into the heart center, accessing the emotions trapped in what William Swygard calls "unfinished business," the residue of life plans left unfulfilled. I place emphasis on the emotional component of the experience when guiding people into their Past lives. I am constantly amazed how quickly they are able to access deeply felt emotional situations, ones that often mirror something happening in their Present life. I have come to realize that this heart-based method is the best way to access and process Past life experiences in our modern age.

It's possible that what I'm exploring now is just as mind-blowing and paradigm-shifting as *running* a Past life was in the 1970s. I am honored to continue the Swygard's work, and hope my story aids you in making progress much faster than I did.

INTRODUCTION

As long as we look at life from the perspective of having only one brief life to live, we can only conceive of a purpose and place for selves in the larger order of things in terms that fit into these few years. From the one-timer's perspective, we are all necessarily reduced to bit parts in life.

Christopher Bache, *Lifecycles: Reincarnation and the Web of Life* [1]

It was after a particularly intense Past lives session that a client alerted me to a realization they perceived: When we first scheduled our session, they experienced the awareness of a flurry of behind-the-scenes activity set in motion, much like a play when an audience gets tickets and takes their seats in the theatre. When the curtain opens to the spotlight shining on the stage, the audience experiences the culmination of countless hours of intricate work by a talented group of professionals covering all aspects of the production—from script, costumes, and sets to casting, rehearsals, lighting, and music.

This client made me aware that our *combined* "behind-the-scenes" creatives—mine as well as theirs—were at work in similar ways. And the "production"—which was our session—was put into motion from the moment they first contacted me for a session, then fully realized when I opened the curtain with my first question.

In a similar way, this book is the "curtain opening" culmination of decades of work in the process I call "Past Life Journeying." In this first volume of a series, my primary mission is to present a new template for the work of Past life study. My goal is to move beyond the old models that utilize long, drawn out hypnotic inductions to a new, 21st century model that functions beautifully for exploring all our "Other" lives—Past, Present, and Future. I present this book as merely the first step in an odyssey of consciousness-expansion while acknowledging the work of familiar past masters such as Brian Weiss, Dolores Cannon, and Michael Newton. Others deserving of greater recognition include Morris Netherton, Roger Woolger, Dick Sutphen, Mary LaBay, Christopher Bache, Bruce Goldberg, and Michael Talbot.

I've read many books on Past lives and I've never found any authors or practitioners who used their own experiences as a basis for discussion. I saw this as an opportunity to show Past Life Journeying in action, so I include as examples my transcripts and notes selected from hundreds of personal sessions in addition to those from my clients.

I'll show you how my introduction to a non-hypnotic method of accessing Past lives launched me into a lifelong inner journey of personal Past- and Between-lives exploration. We'll not only discuss William and Diane Swygard's Awareness Technique, but the history of other practitioners who successfully explored Past lives without the standard hypnotic regression model.

In my journey I eventually discovered one vital clue I missed in my personal sessions…a clue about linear Time and the way it operated. I'll show you how this compelled me to re-examine assumptions about Time through the work of brilliant researchers who completely transformed my awareness of how Time operates. With this new appreciation of Time (now always spelled respectfully with a capital "T"), I adapted the Awareness Technique to journey to my Future lives. I never imagined that this same process which guided me to Past life explorations would work equally well when applied to Future lives.

Finally, I'll give you some insights into my personal practice to help you on your own journey, with tips and suggestions gleaned from decades of experience. I include my expanded version of the original instructions for this method, the Awareness Technique, so that this book can become a guide in your own personal journeys into Past, Between, and Future lives.

I invite you to consider this: information from our various incarnations exists just below the surface of our daily interactions, waiting to be revealed and released. The clues are there if we know how to pay attention; it is there in our phobias and fears, our desires and disappointments, our frustrations and talents. With the tools in this book, you can choose to open your consciousness and release old impulses, heal old wounds, and recover lost skills and abilities. (And maybe even Time travel!)

I also offer *Past Life Journeying* as a tool to those communities involved in the investigation of expanded consciousness who might never consider exploring Past lives: near-death-experience (NDE) researchers, shamanic journeyers, psychonauts, and researchers in the UFO/UAP field open to exploring the consciousness component of the phenomenon. And the best part? It requires no drugs, drumming, almost-dying, or alien abduction.

Here is an example of how I opened a doorway into a field of information for myself when the writing process for this book became bogged down: As I sat down at my laptop, I encountered all my fears, doubts, and worries about having the knowledge and creativity to write this series of books about my ongoing Past and (now) Future lives research. In confronting this mind chatter, I decided to follow the advice I would give to someone else—get a Past lives perspective on the situation.

I followed the instructions (again, included in this book): to expand out of my physical body and allow my energy body to float high up above my house and the body in the chair, with the intention to receive a message of wisdom from a Past life. I did this, then came down to the ground in a previous body from a previous incarnation.

Then I asked myself the curtain-raising first question: "Look down at your feet. What, if anything, are you wearing on your feet?"

I saw an image of sandals made of leather, held on by a strap around my big toe and tied to my ankles. I was walking on sand in daylight. Looking down at the lower part of my body, I saw a billowy fabric— off-white and more of a wrap than a tunic—that also covered my head and shielded my eyes.

When I expanded my awareness to my surroundings, I saw that I was walking toward a village, leading a camel that was carrying much less cargo than I would have expected, just a bag hanging on either side with pockets holding my meager supplies. I had the sense of being an adult male, tall, thin, bearded, and sunbaked with a squint that came from constantly having sand blown in one's eyes.

With a sense of what I was wearing and what I was doing, I accessed the state of this person's inner mind in that moment. I felt that it was surprisingly calm and clear, with the Zen-like mindfulness of living fully in the moment.

I saw myself encountering a collection of tents and was greeted as if I was expected. A man took my camel and led me into a tent, where I was given a cushion to sit upon and some finger food and tea in a small metal cup. (I still love tea after a meal, regardless of the weather. Boiling water poured over leaves or herbs completes every menu for me.)

After the meal, someone came in and sat across from me. There was no physical contact, hand shaking, or hugging as they introduced themselves. Upon hearing the person's name, I started speaking and realized I was conveying a message. They simply nodded when I finished talking, then stood up and left, to be replaced by another person who also sat down and gave me their name.

As people came and went for the rest of that afternoon, I realized that I was the Bedouin version of a mailman (I don't know if that was an exact description, but I use names and titles as placeholders, as you'll see). In my job I moved from village to village delivering news from families, business and trade details, political proclamations, and even marriage proposals with responses.

What was striking is that this person, who was (and is) a part of me, had incredible mental abilities. As soon as a person told me their name, I would start speaking, almost as if I was reading from an inner script; each a bravura performance for an audience of one. My script? Whatever message someone in a previous location had given me, delivered it with whatever emotion was appropriate to convey: sympathetic in delivering a message from parent to child, serious in an offered business deal, authoritative in describing a politician's overture, or poetic in giving or responding to a marriage proposal.

This person's job—my job—was fascinating, especially in the way he was present with each person who sat before him. I became aware of the astounding mental abilities of this "Bedouin Mailman," who used no written notes, only each person's name and location, to trigger his recall. I believe we created computers in the image of our own brains, so I found the mental "hard drive" and "software" that he used in retrieving information astounding. His ability was amazing, not only in remembering these messages, but also recalling and delivering them in the proper context without any obvious order to their conveyance…not to mention the fact that it could have been weeks or months between the stops on his route. He simply retrieved each "file" from his mental hard drive as people came in and introduced themselves. He delivered the message, noting any response before moving on to the next person.

So here I was, in my Present middle-aged body and mind, confronting my insecurities about "delivering this message" to Future readers. My consciousness gave me access to the Previous experience of a man with astonishing mental capacity. If the unspoken question was, "Can I do this creative work?" the answer was being shown my Previous mental and creative capabilities, which remain embedded in my soul's record.

What continues to fascinate me is the backstory I receive in remembering and processing information from a Previous incarnation. Small details, like how I had no attachment to the camel I traveled with. It was like a rental car; I picked it up at one village and traveled with it to the next stop, where I got a fresh one. The clear state of mind that my "Bedouin Mailman" had upon arriving was an indication that he remained ever-present in the moment throughout his journey. His clarity of mind reflected a man not given to ruminating on past failures or missed connections. He retained a clarity of consciousness that I aspire to but do not yet possess (more on that later).

At that moment in my journey of discovery, my higher mind told me I had once possessed creative capability in my Past, and that it was attainable in my Present. With this perspective, I was enlightened by the awareness that in my personal history—and still within me now—I possess the skills and experience needed to successfully convey and express ideas, and to provide others access to an infinite field of information.

This is the intention I have for writing this book: to share information from my decades-long work with the Swygards' Awareness Technique… not only with my experiences, but with my hundreds of clients and the brave participants in the Asheville Past Lives Project over the last few years. And now there are additional adventures I'll be sharing with my recent expansion into Future lives and the process I call Past Life Journeying. Specifically, my concept of "Past" lives has shifted further with additional insight, with a reframing "Past" lives to "Other" or "Adjacent" lives… something we'll explore later in the book.

First up is my origin story—how the discovery of the Awareness Technique launched me on this journey while I was "on the road."

Don't depend on death to liberate you from your imperfections. You are exactly the same after death as you were before. Nothing changes; you only give up the body. If you are a thief or a liar or a cheater before death, you don't become an angel merely by dying. If such were possible, then let us all go and jump in the ocean now and become angels at once! Whatever you have made of yourself thus far, so will you be hereafter. And when you reincarnate, you will bring that same nature with you. To change, you have to make the effort. This world is the place to do it.

Paramahansa Yogananda, *The Divine Romance*[ii]

PART 1:
DISCOVERING
THE AWARENESS
TECHNIQUE

*In which I discover the Awareness Technique
and a Past life on a Texas road trip.*

*I said it in my first book, and it's worth repeating here: anyone
who thinks children are born as blank slates has clearly never been
around one. Your soul comes into each life with plans, goals, and
millennia of experience, like a computer that comes out of the box
loaded with software, games, and apps. With multiple lifetimes
of experience behind it, you'd think your soul would have all the
answers. Sadly, that's not the case. Your soul is on a long journey
here on the earthly plane, coming back time and time again to
pick up new knowledge, and to learn what it is to be human.*[iii]

Ainslie MacLeod in an awesomely titled blog post "Why are Past lives so awful?"

MY ORIGIN STORY

I've had some amazing experiences applying William and Diane Swygard's instructions for exploring Past lives without the traditional hypnotic induction. Working by myself, with members of my Asheville Past Lives Project Meetup here in Western North Carolina, and (eventually) clients all over the world using FaceTime and Zoom technologies, I've become convinced that Past Life Journeying is a powerful tool for expanding consciousness.

First, some background.

As is fitting for someone known as a Past Lives Practitioner, let's look *back* before moving forward. My name (at this time and in this body) is R. C. Baranowski, known to friends and clients as Bobby B. My fascination with exploring Past lives began when I was introduced to the *Awareness Techniques* in the late 1970s.

In addition to my current work as a researcher and facilitator of Past, Between, and Future life explorations, I have been a musician, teacher, writer and metaphysical researcher. I have meditated using a variety of techniques since I was a teenager, starting with transcendental meditation (TM) in college. I later pursued the teachings of Paramahansa Yogananda through the Self-Realization Fellowship and studied with a female Qi Gong master for three years. My personal journeys into higher levels of consciousness have rocked my world to its very foundations…and that's coming from someone who took a much different path to rocking people's worlds.

My first passion was playing the drums, a path I pursued from the first time I sat behind a drum kit at the age of 14. This led to 40+ years of creating, recording, touring, and teaching music. My first love was rock and roll, and I was good enough to play in pre-hipster Brooklyn bars before I was old enough to drink—a 15-year-old kid drumming with older guys my brother's age. I dropped out of college in my early twenties to join a band from Dallas, Texas that moved to New York City in search of a record deal. As a member of "The Werewolves" I became part of the downtown Manhattan club scene when it exploded in the late 1970s.

Lower Manhattan was dangerous, dirty, and a lot more fun then. It was an amazing music scene: playing gigs at now-legendary clubs like CBGB and Max's Kansas City, living at the Chelsea Hotel, getting (and losing) a major label record deal, and working with a superstar manager/producer. I experienced 13 of my 15 minutes of fame when our first album was released. But that ended when the label dropped us after our second album was recorded (but not yet released). Seeking a new record deal, the band moved to Los Angeles, then back to New York City, where we broke up. I followed the bass player back to Dallas and, after his untimely death, learned how to play blues with schooling from some of the best musicians in Dallas and Austin.

It was an amazing journey. I played anywhere anyone would hire me: from clubs with deafening volume to restaurants where the band had to be quiet enough for diners to converse, from biker bars to country dance halls, from Dallas' Deep Ellum to Austin's famed Antone's blues club and at the Rock & Roll Hall of Fame induction for Buddy Holly (with one of his former bandmates). I moved around the country, bouncing between New York, Dallas, Austin, and Los Angeles, working odd jobs to support my music habit. I painted houses and mowed lawns. I drove equipment trucks in the NYC film and television industry. I even worked as a "lot dog" at one of the studios in LA, where one of my jobs was sweeping the set of the TV game show *Jeopardy*.

You may not have heard of me—or any of the incredibly talented musicians with whom I played and recorded—in spite of decades spent seeking fame and fortune. Such is the life of a journeyman musician…or at least it was, until years of ear-splitting volume took its toll on my hearing and tinnitus ended my ability to play music. (As I write this, my ears are ringing loud enough to wake the neighbors.)

On vacation from that truck-driving job in Brooklyn, I discovered the peace and beauty of Asheville, North Carolina. I moved here in 2014, seeking to reinvent myself in another creative career. In the quiet of the Blue Ridge mountains, I resumed an exploration of Past lives and had a series of paradigm-shattering experiences. These brought me to the realization that a parallel passion for metaphysical research and spiritual progress was becoming my primary focus.

I wanted to deeply explore the Awareness Technique, and its non-hypnotic method of accessing Past lives, with the goal of "seeing through the eyes and hearing through the ears" of a Past life personality. I wondered if it were possible to refine this 1960s technique for our modern era and energy. In 2016 I organized the Asheville Past Lives Project Meetup, which gave me the opportunity to connect with others interested in, or experienced with, Past lives.

Finally, I began holding one-on-one client sessions. One of my first was with an Asheville woman who referred me to her mother, who lived across the country. I realized that, with an internet connection, I could guide a Past life session with anyone, anywhere in the world. That led me to create my PastLivesProject.org website, which holds my blog, workshops, presentations, the Inner-Views/interview series with practitioners and artists, and—now—to this book.

FROM SKEPTIC TO ENTHUSIAST

How does a musician expand his consciousness when he moves from Brooklyn to the mountains of Western North Carolina? My journey from skeptic to enthusiast began when I walked into a bookstore and found Page Bryant's book, *The Spiritual Reawakening of the Great Smoky Mountains*. I thought I was open-minded in my search for answers when I found this guidebook describing the history, secrets, and energy centers of the beautiful mountains to which I'd just moved. Perfect, I thought. But as I stood at the counter waiting to pay, I read that Bryant's spirit guide, "Albion," channeled the information in the book,

"Not for me," I thought as I closed the book, returned it to its shelf, and left the store empty-handed. Maybe it was from having spent the last seven years in the very concrete reality of NYC traffic seen through the windshield of a truck, but I simply was not open to "channeled" information, not yet. But I was still intrigued. I googled the author's name and discovered Page Bryant formerly lived in Sedona, Arizona. In fact, it was she who first wrote about its now-famous vortexes. All the widely accepted information about the area's vortexes was channeled by the spirit guide Albion, which meant that Sedona's entire tourist industry due to those vortexes—including their mention on the home page of the Sedona Visitors Bureau website—is based on channeled information! This was the first of many opportunities I had to re-visit my resistance to channeled wisdom from non-physical sources.

Soon after this, I started attending Jubilee!, an established and very popular non-denominational church in downtown Asheville. Jubilee!

features a different artist each month in their lobby and gives them an opportunity to introduce themselves, so when artist Scott Guynup asked us to check out the books of his wife, Page, I thought, "Hmm...Page... author...small world." It was only when I went to see Scott's awesome art that I also saw *The Spiritual Reawakening of the Great Smoky Mountains* on a table with Page's other books. "Message received!" I thought and met Page that day. I bought a copy of her book, attended some of her talks, and saw her regularly at Jubilee! services until her death in 2017.

There's been a constant unfolding in my spiritual progress since moving to Asheville. When I arrived, I was not open to channeled information; now I can honestly say that some of my favorite people are channelers. In the same way, I originally was not open to Future life explorations, even after reading books on the subject by Bruce Goldberg and Brian Weiss; now it's at the core of my new practice, TimeLine Journeying.

As for the topic of hypnosis, I've gone back and forth. I follow the arguments that now, more than ever, our daily life is filled with trance states, especially with the advent of smart phones continuously hijacking our attention. But the people who initially inspired me, William and Diane Swygard (more on their Awareness Technique in the next chapter), were very anti-hypnosis, believing that it *"takes away consciousness as well as energy from the life function."*[iv] I don't subscribe to that idea, but I *am* someone who cannot be hypnotized (one of as many as 25% of the population cannot be hypnotized, according to Stanford University's Dr. David Spiegel[v]).

My clients are drawn to me because of my non-hypnosis guided meditation approach, but I appreciate that some people prefer the traditional hypnotic regression process. I see it as gaining access to Past lives through a different doorway. Whatever it takes, as long as you're willing to go through that doorway. (And, like channelers, some of my favorite people doing this work are hypnotists.)

My belief as of this writing—always subject to change with further research, but based on my personal experience—is that it is not necessary to enter into a deep hypnotic trance to access Past lives. Hans TenDam, author of the encyclopedic *Exploring Reincarnation: The Classic Guide to the Evidence for Past Lives*, noted this also:

> *Most people who try easily get impressions from previous lives, often quite vivid and quite remarkable, often with interesting results. Hypnotic regression has long been the main tool for recall, but it is rapidly being replaced by methods that avoid, or employ only weak, trance induction, sometimes enabling people to have vivid recall of pastlife episodes within a few minutes.*[vi]

It's been over 50 years since the Swygards first published *The Awareness Techniques*, and many decades since Brian Weiss and Michael Newton published their groundbreaking works. Thousands, if not millions, of open-minded individuals have been exposed to the concept of Past lives through books, movies, YouTube videos, and—now—webinars. I firmly believe, and have seen in my own practice, that information from Past lives is more readily available to our conscious mind now than it was when this field's seminal works were written decades ago. I recall being astonished the first time I helped a small group of people in my Meetup "dip their toes" into a Past life experience. Using a positive emotional experience as a bridge, I took them on the journey and brought them back...all in 15 minutes, and without hypnosis!

It's possible I'm perceiving what Past Lives Regression Academy founder Andy Tomlinson noticed:

> *I am aware that the vibrations of earth have risen since 2012, as the veil to the spirit world has thinned and new and deeper information about the soul is becoming available.*[vii]

My approach applies two of the most powerful words in the English language: "what" and "if."

> What if...instead of using hypnotic trance to disconnect our conscious mind, we use focusing techniques to expand awareness and take our conscious mind *with* us on the journey?

> What if...we use our conscious mind as a reference when exploring how the people, places, and things in our Past lives resonate with our Present life?

> What if...with this enhanced awareness, we open ourselves to the possibility that Time does not function the way we've been led to believe?

> What if...the reason Past (and Future) lives echo in our Present life is because they are running "Adjacent" to our Present life, i.e.: happening at the same time?

> What if...there is a next step forward and the same methods allowing us to explore Past lives can be utilized to give us access to Future timelines?

These "what if" questions and much more will be explored in this book. But first, some background on the incredibly innovative method that launched my explorations, the Awareness Technique.

> *All human beings should try to learn before they die*
> *what they are running from, and to, and why.*
>
> James Thurber, writer and cartoonist (1894-1961) [viii]

THE AWARENESS TECHNIQUE

The Awareness Techniques are tools...questions are the motivating factors in the use of the technique...(and) only a question or desire can put these tools to work. When the question is asked or a desire to know is manifest...the "running" of the answer to your question or desire will continue only as long as it takes to answer the question or desire. Then, the answer manifestation will discontinue. It shuts off. It takes another question or desire to motivate the integrated consciousness* tool further.

William Swygard, *Awareness Techniques – Book 1*[ix]
*(Swygard describes an "integrated consciousness" as one who is connected to multiple levels of consciousness through the practice of this procedure.)

I began exploring Past lives when I was introduced to the work of William and Diane Swygard, a couple who operated a Miami, Florida bookstore in the 1960s. Beginning in 1970, they published a series of pamphlets beginning with *Awareness Techniques – Book 1*. The introduction, dated 1968, describes how this non-hypnotic technique *"...has been tested in all of its aspects upon persons of various races, religious backgrounds, and ages for over eighteen years in the Miami, Florida area."*[x]

There were four pamphlets in the *Awareness Techniques* series, each describing a further application of the work. (I have not deeply explored the other techniques. Possibly due to their extremely esoteric nature, they are rarely referenced.) The Swygards also published three pamphlets in the

Waldara Answers series, which functioned as question-and-answer FAQs for the use of the technique. ("Waldara" is William Swygard's spirit name, which we'll talk about later.)

William Swygard started pursuing this work in the late 1940s. In 2018 I spoke to Diane Swygard Harper, who told me that William wrote his part of the books by hand, and that she then edited, typed, and even typeset the manuscript prior to publication. No mystery school was established, no subscriptions written.

In the pre-internet era, they placed ads in the classified section of *Fate Magazine* inviting people to send a stamped, self-addressed envelope to the Miami address. By return mail, they would send the instructions for what they called *"running"* Past lives as a simple sheet of paper folded into four sections. William, who had been in the film business in Miami, possibly chose the metaphor of a film strip to view a Past life...as in "running" a film strip through a projector, complete with the ability to stop, freeze a frame, rewind, or fast forward. One of the participants in those early sessions was Helen Hoag, who described this process:

> *You can "run" your past lives, as the process is called because it is like a motion picture "running" through a projection machine.*[xi]

By William Swygard's account, they printed and mailed 10,000 copies of these instructions for *running* Past lives, some of them outside of the United States.

I learned the technique from two Dallas friends, who received their copy of the instructions in the mail and started *running* sessions together. These two friends, Paul Newell and Miguel Paredes, became adept at what they called The Technique and taught it to me when I was playing gigs in Texas in the late 1970s. When I moved to Dallas in the 1980s, Paul and I pursued the work more intensely, even communicating with Diane Swygard.

The Awareness Technique process opens with a few guided exercises to stretch the participant out of the physical body into what the Swygards called "the etheric body." Then we move the etheric body up and out of the physical arena to explore the physical space outside the body, sending this etheric body to the roof of the building which the participant occupies in this Present life. From there we ascend 500 feet in the air while looking down, learning to navigate outside the physical body while answering questions.

Quite the feat of coordination! Only when the participant learns how to navigate with their etheric body do we move back down into a Previous incarnation of the physical body, descending firmly but gently to stand on the ground in that Past life physical body. When the participant feels their feet on the ground, we ask them to look down and describe what, if anything, they are wearing on those feet, either by seeing, feeling, or (for some people) asking themselves, "What am I wearing on my feet?" From the original instructions by William and Diane Swygard: *Please look down at your feet and tell me what you are wearing on your feet.*[xii] (It was only after doing sessions in Asheville that I had to include the words "if anything" because so many people reported being barefoot!)

Despite intensive research, I have not discovered any printed material utilizing the "look down at your feet" instructions before the 1970 publication of *The Awareness Techniques – Book 1*. This was the first clue that, rather than disappearing, some aspects of the Awareness Technique have been absorbed into the more common mainstream hypnotic regression methods in use. For example, even the wikiHow.com post for "Remembering Your Past Lives" utilizes this starting point:

> *...try the shoe method: look down at your feet and go with the first pair of shoes you see yourself wearing, and work from there. You might see sandals, and then realize you're wearing a tunic. You might see*

little pointy shoes and realize you're wearing a big
silk gown.[xiii]

My research into various methods of accessing Past lives (most of which use the standard hypnotic regression technique) revealed that at some point almost all use the instruction to *"look down at what you are wearing on your feet."* The Awareness Technique innovated the language in providing these instructions to establish the participant in their Past life physical body.

It is incredible how much information comes to the surface when a participant identifies their footwear or sees their bare feet. Male or female, young or old, rich or poor, native or city person...all of this comes into awareness when the participant "looks out through the eyes and listens through the ears" using this technique.

Then we move on to the question, "What are you wearing on the lower part of your body?" More information as the physical body emerges and presents itself. Then, "What are you wearing, if anything, on the upper part of your body?" Once again, the words "if anything" allow for a lack of clothing for tropical or primitive lifetimes. More information, more awareness of the physical being and the timeframe in which they live. More of the personality emerges with the outfit. Then, "Is this a male or female body? What is the age range of this body? Is it a child, adolescent, adult, middle age, or elder?"

The next instruction is to, "Look down and tell me where you are standing. Is it day or night? Are you indoors or outdoors?" I ask the participant to expand their awareness to their surroundings as the Past life body becomes established in a physical environment. Indoors or outside, wet or dry, dirt or grass or concrete...each description gives us more information about the Past life that guides us to the personality we uncover.

One question not included in the original instructions that I often ask is this: "Look down at your hands. Are those indoor hands or outdoor hands?" A wealth of detailed information comes from establishing the difference between the smooth hands of someone who has a maid or who works indoors at their desk and the rough, calloused hands of a farmer, blue-collar laborer, or miner. Another important detail is to ask, "Do you see any jewelry—any rings or bracelets? Do they have any significance?"

Knowing what the Past life personality is feeling is the next important detail. I ask, "What is your emotional state of mind?" As occurred during one memorable Past lives session, there is a difference between the experience of a young girl running through a field with joy and the emotional upheaval of being chased by people trying to kill her and her family.

I love the idea that it takes a question to motivate an answer, but that the energy stops until another question puts it back in play. As the facilitator or guide, this is my part in the process—finding the open-ended questions that move the participant smoothly through their Past life experience using the intention the client sets up before the session. (More of this process later.) Swygard explains questions and links them to another important concept: unfinished business.

> *It seems that questions are stimulated into being in our consciousness by a lack of understanding (love) when an unclear situation arises. As the situation passes and the question remains unanswered, a certain amount of awareness remains bound to the question in the remembered situation. The amount of awareness polarized to the unanswered question is equivalent to the amount of awareness-energy necessary to answer the question or solve the problem. The more unfinished business we accumulate, the more awareness (and consciousness) we have bound to the unfinished incidents, and it becomes unavailable to conduct our present and future activities.*[xiv]

Swygard proposes that by asking questions and *running* these "unclear situations" which echo into our Present life, we free up the energy locked behind unfinished business from our Past lives. He also equates unfinished business with karma, which the Oxford English Dictionary defines as "*(in Hinduism and Buddhism) the sum of a person's actions in this and previous states of existence, viewed as deciding their fate in future existences.*"[xv]

> Most important of all, when you can realize the imperfectness and "unfinished business" (sometimes called karma) of your past incarnations, it is easy to "forgive and forget" these actions through self-realization on a mental-spiritual level, and absolve yourself of further action in that regard. This means that you will have completed any "unfinished business" through the highest level of awareness, and will not have to work it out on the slow, painful, unaware level of physical consciousness.[xvi]

Unfortunately, William Swygard passed away in 1981 at the age of 58, before this method of *running* Past lives without the use of hypnotic induction could become commonly accepted. With five of the couple's eleven children still at home, Diane carried on for a while. But the books and the Technique faded into obscurity.

Or so I thought.

Surprisingly, an offshoot known as the "Christos Technique" gained prominence, which used the exact same instructions distributed by the Swygards. According to HypnoticWorld.com: "*The Christos Technique is thought to have originated in Australia with the Open Mind society.*"[xvii]

Not!

In researching the Christos material, I learned that an Australian man by the name of Stanley Spencer learned the Awareness Technique in Miami, most likely from William Swygard himself:

> This technique for recalling details of past incarnations is basically a very simple one. I discovered it

while I was in Miami last year and have used it with
reasonable success on a number of people since. It
involves a series of mental exercises—under direction
from someone (who should be, I feel, a sympathetic
listener and a good questioner).[xviii]

And this from Jaqueline Parkhurst, author of *Altered States of*
Consciousness and the Christos Technique:

The Christos Experiment was adapted by my husband
and I from a method originally outlined by Mr. W.
Swygard of Florida, U.S.A. He was using his method
to remember past lives (or incarnations) and to induce
what he called Multi-Level Awareness.[xix]

("Multi-level awareness" is how *Book 1* describes *running* Past lives
to distinguish it from other processes described in *Books 2, 3,* and *4*.)

Despite extensive research, I've never been able to determine why the
name of the Awareness Technique was changed to the Christos Method,
but to this day it has a larger internet presence than the original Awareness
Technique. With this book I hope to change that and I'm pleased to know
my website, PastLivesProject.com, comes up on the first page of Google
searches for the Awareness Technique and Past lives, directing credit to
the Swygards' innovations.

I noticed another missed opportunity to properly credit the Awareness
Technique when I found this on a YouTube channel which collected the
recordings of Past lives practitioner Dick Sutphen, whose work I'll talk
about in a later chapter:

I call the technique used in the album "The Ascension
Technique" because it requires you to imagine or
fantasize that you are ascending to the top of a house
or the building you are in, and then to a height of 500
feet in the air before receiving special instructions to

descend into a Past life. Now, I understand that a variation of the technique was developed in the mid-1960s and used by a few practitioners who became very excited about the dependability of the method. I first became aware of it in the mid-1970s and began to use it experimentally, especially as an alternative astral projection technique. Over the years, it has been one of many variations of Past life regression I've used in seminars. And again, I've always liked it because it always seemed to work for everybody. Now neither I nor several friends who conduct regressions know exactly why the technique is so effective, and I guess it doesn't really matter. What you are interested in are results.[xx]

Compare this to the instructions in *The Awareness Techniques* where the client is instructed to stand in front of the building where he lives and describe the door, doorknob, windows, etc.:

After he sees and describes to you these objects, tell him to, "Go quickly and stand on the roof of the building and look down into the road (or yard) in front. Tell me as soon as you are there." Ask him to see and describe such objects as cars, road, trees, etc. When this is completed, tell him to go about 500 feet up into the air and look down. (One in a hundred may object at this point but remind him quickly that he is still safe in the room.) Then repeat the request, "Tell me as soon as you are there."[xxi]

It appears that Dick Sutphen was working in the Southwestern U.S. as the same time the Parkhursts were working in Australia. Both were among many practitioners familiar with the Awareness Technique. This lends more credibility to my belief that the original instructions were making the rounds within the community of people pursuing Past lives, since Sutphen also mentions "several friends who conduct regressions." But no one credited the authors William and Diane Swygard, even as they recommended versions of this induction. I'm a fan of Dick Sutphen's work, so I'm not trying to discredit him. I count myself as one of those utilizing the Awareness Technique who, as Sutphen observes, "liked it because it always seemed to work for everybody."

One concept from the Awareness Technique I found most enlightening is in regards to our soul's origin story, which I think of as the "spiritual Big Bang":

> *In the Central Universe, the Creator is at the very center. This is His headquarters and the fountainhead of His awareness. From this center, He releases Spirits...which are part of Him...(E)ach is given a name. They are admonished, by name, to, "Go know My Creation, and return It to me." From this command, they gain more consciousness...*[xxii]

So, in the Swygard's cosmology, all of us are individualized aspects of the Creator, we are here in physical form to experience and/or create, and by this experiencing/creating we gain more consciousness and add to the knowledge of the Creator. This concept was very important in my development because it allowed me to switch from a "what am I here to learn?" approach to a "what can I create from where I am now?" approach.

Another practitioner who may have been acquainted with the Awareness Technique is hypnotherapist Dolores Cannon. I've listened to Dolores Cannon's talks on her YouTube channel and experienced Past life sessions with her Quantum Healing Hypnosis Technique (QHHT) method. I must admit I really enjoy watching someone from my mother's generation talk about Past lives, communication with Nostradamus, and lives on planets other than the "Earth School" (while patting her perm). This quote jumped out of her lecture and perfectly aligns with the Awareness Technique:

> *God was this huge, bright light. And…he was lonely, he wanted to create others. This is when he burst out, this is the "Big Bang" theory, when he burst out into millions and billions of particles. Now when I take you back to what you really are, all you are is a tiny little spark of light; a tiny little spark, that's all you are. So, at that point they all shot out in all directions. Some of these little sparks became planets, some became galaxies, and many of them became individual souls. I have many clients who ask, "I want to know where I came from." Well, we all came from the same place…they all came from God, from the Source, and when they shot out, it was like God said, "Go and learn, my children, learn everything you can and bring it back to me."* [xxiii]

Now, I have no idea if Dolores Cannon ever heard of the Awareness Technique, but it's even more astounding if the information she got from her source led her to the same concept as William and Diane Swygard. Look at how closely these two quotes line up:

> Cannon: *Go and learn, my children, learn everything you can and bring it back to me.*

> William and Diane Swygard: *Go, know My Creation, and return it to Me.*

Either way, this powerful concept influenced my life and work.

Also note that each individual component of Source is given a name when released. For example, according to *Awareness Techniques – Book 1*, William Swygard's Spirit name is "Waldara." When Paul Newell and I were in communication with Diane Swygard in the 1980s, she advised us to ask for my Spirit name while *running* a Past life. She wisely thought it more important for us to learn it for ourselves rather than hear it from an outside source.

I asked for my Spirit name when *running* a Past life, which she affirmed for me, and I have used it as my personal guide stone ever since. My Spirit name is "Ramta-Anda." Unfortunately there is a spiritual entity named Ramtha, channeled by J. Z. Knight with "his" own School of Enlightenment, so to avoid confusion I've kept it to myself until now.

RUNNING A PAST LIFE

I've always loved the use of the word *running* to describe the process of the Awareness Technique; I've been using it for over 40 years and it fits perfectly. The "film" is our Past life experience, and *running* is the viewing of that experience. (And yes, I recognize "film" as a pre-digital image. But as I said earlier: just go with it! Film looks better anyway.) Film is viewed by running it past a light source. During the session the participant holds the piece of film with their Past life information on it, and as they *run* the film through the light source of consciousness, they can stop at any point and freeze a frame to examine it closely. They can go backward or fast forward, or even access a different film strip entirely; the participant is in complete control of viewing what is recorded.

After working together, one of my clients recommended her daughter for a session. She didn't want to give her any details, opting to compare notes after both of them had the experience. But the mother did tell her daughter to "bring a box of tissues." As I mentioned before there *is*, in fact, emotional information stored in our Past lives which remains very close to the surface, waiting to be released. Often the first event that arises in a session is intensely emotional. I believe this technique is incredibly powerful at accessing and releasing those trapped emotions, or *unfinished business*, and that powerful healing is possible when those emotions are freed.

My first rule for this process is to never re-traumatize anyone. I start every session with the participant by setting an intention or asking a question to guide us on our exploration. I make certain the participant knows they have the option to stop any scene directed to them by their consciousness, either by shifting awareness to look at the scene from above (thereby allowing them to access information from the situation without emotional involvement) or by moving to another lifetime and starting the process again. The participant is always in control, and this is reinforced before the session starts.

You don't have to *run* the experience of having your head on the chopping block (been there!) for it to be traumatizing. A client was describing a seemingly normal medieval dinner party in detail when they became distressed and didn't want to see any more. In such a case, I ask them to put a bookmark in this scene, then allow themselves to float up in the air once again. They were guided back down to earth to a different lifetime and had a very satisfactory session.

I also do sessions with people to reclaim unused abilities and personal powers they feel are restricted. The "Inner-View" interview series on my website (PastLivesProject.org/plp-innerviews) features practitioners exploring their Past (and Adjacent) personalities who were involved in their art or healing practice, with fascinating results. (The first series of Inner-Views was conducted before my Time awakening, when I was still working from the assumption that our lives proceed in a linear manner. I plan to do more of these interviews, and it will be interesting to see how simultaneous and non-linear Time factor into the progression of people's talents and abilities…and of course, what form these creative and healing passions take in their Future lives.)

What most amazes me is how unique every participant experience is. Maybe it's because I'm working from the heightened energies of these magnificent Blue Ridge mountains, but I do not see a "scripted" format, either in sessions or Between lives, as some people claim in the more popular books written on this subject. There are some similarities between sessions, but each participant is encouraged to find their own way through their Past lives and their own distinct transition from the physical to the non-physical experience Between lives. I'll talk more on that in the next section, but first, a *Running* Tip about costumes.

> *Have you heard about "unfinished business"?*
> *It's finished, you just didn't like the way it came out.*

Richard Bandler, *Using Your Brain for a Change*[xxiv]

RUNNING TIP: COSTUMES

What if we are more than this present-day body, mind, history, and story? What if beyond the ego-ic [sic] drives of fear and gain, that we are in essence, really beings of love? What if this experience that we call life is really just a semester of Earth school? And that in between these semesters of Earth school, there's a realm that we can go to...a realm that is of great beauty, creativity, connection...a realm with humor, of learning...a realm of great peace and love? What if beyond the costumes of this life there is another and a larger story of who we are?

Richard Martini, *It's a Wonderful Afterlife*[xxv]

Inspired by the directions in the Awareness Technique instructions: *Look down at what you are wearing on your feet*, I have explored how the clothing with which we've chosen to cover our bodies—at any point in our vast history, even in the present day—can be seen as costumes. And if our physical existence is really "just a play," as one participant described their experience, then we might also describe ourselves as actors on a stage.

With that perspective, the clothing we put on this morning is as much of a "costume" as that of a medieval jester, a cloistered monk, a soldier in World War I, an ancient Egyptian priest, or even the skins and hides covering a caveman's back. All of these are costumes I wore in the Previous lives I've explored. When I dress each morning and put on my Asheville uniform of jeans, t-shirt, and hiking shoes, I wonder how today's "costumes" will appear when I look back on this Present life from the distant future, possibly when we're all wearing form-fitting Star Trek-style uniforms. In my Meetups, I guided a group meditation to acquaint people with the costumes they were wearing, first with eyes open, and then with closed-eyed awareness:

> Start with your Present-day costume. With eyes open, look down at your feet and describe what you are wearing as if you are giving information to someone who is sketching you without seeing you. How would you describe the cloth, rubber, plastic, or leather that covers your feet? What are you wearing on the lower part of your body? Is it a pair of pants or a skirt that proceeds from the waist, or is it something that hangs from the upper body or shoulders? What is covering the upper part of your body? Is it long-sleeved or short? Are the sleeves buttoned at the wrist? Does it have a collar? Is it open at the neck? How would you describe your hair: long or short? Dark or light? Curly or straight? Is there any ornamentation at the neck or ears...any necklace or earrings? Any bracelets on the wrist or rings on the fingers? Is there an emotional connection to this jewelry or is it just ornamentation? Now close your eyes and feel what is covering your body. Feel what is covering your feet, your lower body, your waist, your upper body, your arms, and around your neck. Feel your hair (or lack of it) and whether anything is covering your head.

Becoming aware of what we're wearing in our Present-day body is a good warmup for the *running* process, especially for people who are not especially visual. If you can't see what you're wearing with your eyes closed, maybe you can *feel* what you're wearing. If you can't feel, try asking for a verbal prompt and see if you get a reply; sometimes that will kickstart the visuals. (This is how I work when exploring in my own sessions, as I am not especially visual.) Knowing your predominant sensory modality—visual, kinetic, tactile, auditory, emotional, or some combination—is helpful in your inner journeys.

Now go about your day and notice how many costumes you see on other people. As you walk around your city or town, can you tell the difference between tourists and the locals by their costumes? See these as the costumes of goths and jocks, businesspeople and hippies, soldiers and clergy, high-society types and farm hands. Our costumes are both socially defined and socially defining. They are crowd-sanctioned, with social credit for participating "correctly" and points off for defying the norm.

Think renaissance fairs and American civil war reenactments, which are socially acceptable opportunities to wear costumes from previous eras. (The son of one friend practices English country dancing from the 19th century with his girlfriend, using full period costume.) I will be the last to judge anyone else's costumes, especially when there are promotional pictures of me in full 70s and 80s rock-band regalia on the internet (which will surely outlast any nuclear event along with cockroaches).

But this is not an exercise in fashion; this is practice for *running* the first step of the Awareness Technique for a Past life. As you look down at your feet and then describe your body coverings in detail, a personality eventually emerges, and the person behind those clothes is acknowledged. Clothes are the pathway to the inner life of the actor on the stage. Become aware of the costume you wear today and use it as a bridge to examine your role in the play that is your Present life.

One of my most visual Past life identities was the street performer I call the "Jongleur." According to the Merriam-Webster dictionary, a jongleur is "an itinerant medieval entertainer proficient in juggling, acrobatics, music, and recitation." Interestingly, I knew what a jongleur was because one of my best friends in college was an actor in a theater group called "The Jongleurs." They practiced a multitude of skills including mime, juggling, and acrobatics much like an ancient street troupe. This is another example of how our Past lives "echo" into our Present life in interesting ways.

> Looking down at my feet, I'm wearing pointy shoes with bells on the tip, balloon pants, a puffy shirt that ties at the neck, a beard, and a long, droopy jester's hat. I anger a nobleman with a joke, and one of his bodyguards puts a long, thin sword through my left cheek. Lots of blood. I had it wrapped and was planning to leave because I could no longer work in that nobleman's area. Then I received word they were coming to arrest me, which was much worse than to coming to kill me. I wrote this down because it was so poetic: "I am leaving, and the only direction is away."
> I fled through the forest at night. When I came to a river, I got in and floated as long as I could. I finally pulled myself on shore, sick with fever from an infection, shivering. People came and put a blanket on me. I woke up hallucinating that my helpers were witches, jumped back into the water to escape, and drowned.

Next up: an exploration of the Between lives state I call the Non-Physical Experience.

> *(W)e must come to understand that the stages we mark from the cradle to the grave constitute only ½ of the human life cycle. There is a second half of the cycle that is not being considered but must be addressed if we want to appreciate the large rhythm of human existence...Reincarnation does not make much sense if we try to understand only in terms of physical existence...The spiritual (non-physical) phase of our life is as important to our development as our earthly phase is.*

Christopher Bache, *Lifecycles: Reincarnation and the Web of Life*[xxvi]

DYING AND THE NON-PHYSICAL EXPERIENCE BETWEEN LIVES

I believe we bring unconscious awareness of the events of our past lives with us throughout our life experience. I believe that when the body dies, consciousness continues to exist and relocates or reincarnates into a new body in a circle of life. Just as a graduation is also a commencement, so death is also the beginning of a new cycle of life.

Bernie Siegel, MD, in a foreword to *Invisible Roots - How Healing Past Life Trauma Can Liberate Your Present* [xxvii]

There is one constant if you were ever incarnated in a different physical body: Spoiler alert! that physical body died. In my sessions I can easily get participants to journey to a Past life. And at the end of that life we proceed to their transition out of the body: the death experience. I make a point of reminding people that they have probably lived a few—possibly dozens, maybe even hundreds or even thousands—of Past lives with one thing in common: every single one of those lives ended…sometimes alone and suffering but still holding onto life, other times surrounded by family and ready to release the body. And when they died, at some point (but not always immediately), their spirit separated from their body and they experienced an interlude outside of time and the physical world…the Between lives state that I call the Non-Physical Experience.

A very important part of this work is discovering what the Past life personality experienced emotionally in the moments before death. I agree with other researchers that this transition is extremely important:

One's thoughts at the moment of death have a powerful effect on mediating the inheritance from one life to another. In these moments we either make our peace with our life as it was or carry our lack of peace forward to work out later.

Christopher Bache, *Lifecycles: Reincarnation and the Web of Life*[xxviii]

It is in the moments before death—often when we realize death is imminent, but also when it occurs unexpectedly—that we find important information about that life:

- whether we are at peace or filled with regrets (regardless of physical pain)

- our awareness of unfinished business from that life and what was left undone

- our vows to do something different next time if given the chance (or even vows of revenge on whoever we feel harmed us or our loved ones)

- upon exiting a life with its significant personalities, how it resonates with our Present life

These and other "death-bed issues" leave a massive imprint upon our energy fields and carry over more intensely than issues from earlier in life.

I access this state with the prompt: *Go to your last day in that life. Where are you and what is going on around you?* After establishing where we are and who is with us (if anyone) we connect to the mental and emotional state of our Past life personality, paying particular attention to whether we feel at peace or overwhelmed by unfinished business from that life, whether we accept our passing (justified or not), or even if we vow revenge on the perpetrator who interrupted our life's journey. Then we move to the "in-between" lives state, the Non-Physical Experience or NPE, which can be accessed as simply as continuing the question-and-answer process, asking, *What happens next?* or even more precisely, *What is the next significant event?*

But the transition to the Between lives state is not a digital, on/off process. We can remain connected in varying degrees to the body we inhabited, the life we lived, and the people we left behind. Some clients have reported transitions where they lingered, giving another context to the reports of ghosts "visiting" loved ones after passing:

- After dying in a shipwreck, one person waited for someone to discover their body and bury it before leaving.

- One mother immediately checked in with their son (who was ill), waited with him until he died, and left together with him.

- In my own World War I life where I died very unexpectedly at age 19, I immediately checked in with my wife, who was pregnant when I left to join the military. It was only when I saw that the child, whom I never met, was being cared for by my wife's family that I left the physical plane.

Other times, the transition occurs instantly:

- My World War II life was short and I desperately wanted out of my starving, brutalized body. I *ran* my transition, trying to float upwards, but felt like I was "stuck"…as if something was holding me to the physical plane. It was only when a literal helping hand reached out and lifted me up that I was able to float upwards and away from that life. (Floating upward is the most common experience described to me by my clients.)

- My "unplanned exit" example below is one where I couldn't wait to detach from the body and didn't look back.

This Between lives, non-physical continuity of consciousness is where the most powerful work occurs when we are ready and willing to deeply explore something that was not a point of emphasis in Swygards' original instructions. Although *Book 1* did recommend *running* at least 20 lives before advancing to their other techniques, there were no specific instructions for the Between lives experience. Hypnotherapist Michael Newton is credited with introducing this concept to a wider audience with his 1994 book, *Journey of Souls – Case Studies of Life Between Lives*. Learning to "navigate" this Between lives state outside the physical body can be an intense spiritual experience, as statements from my clients show. This also opens the Time door, since experiences of the Non-Physical realm also exist outside of linear Time, as we shall see in later chapters.

I offer my Past life facilitating experience as an alternative to Michael Newton's more well-known "Life Between Lives" method. I have yet to experience a session with Newton's technique, as I am not a good hypnotic subject despite multiple attempts with highly trained professionals. I also do much better with a 75- or 90-minute format as opposed to his three-and-a-half to five-hour LBL sessions.

My goal is to allow each journeyer to have their own unique experience in the Between lives realm without expecting a whole checklist of "events" to follow: the life review, the meeting with the "council," and the planning session with guides for the next life. (I can always tell when clients have read *Journey of Souls*; they have expectations of going through this "checklist.") I advise clients to treat any Between lives "review process" not as a judgmental external report card, but as more of an internal performance review. I believe we all have our own path to follow, and my aim is to provide the guidance to open that pathway.

One significant experience I had in my own Between lives session was an "unplanned exit" from a life as a particularly nasty businessman. This was an opportunity to experience a Past personality as the perpetrator instead of the victim, as we'll see in a later chapter. This Past life, whom I dubbed the "Greedy Bastard," allowed me insight into the mind of someone who possessed immense wealth along with horrific selfishness, i.e.: "If I give you a penny, that means I have one penny less." He was arrogant enough to think cheating his crooked partners—who were basically pirates—was a good idea. That led to the following visual:

> I was leaving my office on the docks when someone came up from behind and slit my throat. As I lay on the damp ground, my attacker reached into my pocket, found my purse, and rained the coins down on my dying body. From my notes on that session: "I exited that body like an actor leaving the stage, tearing off the wardrobe and makeup of the villain in a soap opera."

I assume this was a "lesson learned" situation. I recall my soul's revulsion at being that personality, an instance of leaving a life with deep regret for my behavior. My experience resonated with clients who also use the metaphor of a stage show in describing their experience. In fact, the most common reaction from participants navigating to this Between lives state is, "It's just a play."

I've had the good fortune to take many clients into the Between lives experience (and I include my own below). I'm privileged to hear their stories and ask them questions when they are in the state of consciousness beyond day-to-day reality. The wisdom they impart opens my mind and heart. There are tears—sometimes my own—as I listen to these amazing stories. Some people's experiences are very ephemeral, requiring metaphor and poetry to describe the non-physical: being surrounded by entities like "smoky ghosts" is a favorite description. Others are very rooted in the physicality of the life just left. One client described being an old widower who spent his final days missing his wife after her passing. When the old man died, his transitional state began on a dance floor, wearing his favorite cowboy boots and dancing with his wife, reunited.

Wisdom from Between Lives Sessions

Clients often reveal next-level wisdom in their sessions, which I am infinitely grateful and privileged to receive in answer to the questions I pose in the course of those sessions. This is a chapter of that wisdom taken from client sessions.

One participant talked about "The Unity," a state where there are no individual souls, where all are blended into a collective. According to this participant, in this place individual experiences are "uploaded" to the collective experience for "processing."

Others also experience this communal aspect. One participant told me, "We're all one until we decide to come back," into another physical body. "They greet me, they bring me in, we merge. All the information from that life…melds with everyone…not just what I thought or felt. It's all sensory input—taste, touch, smell; they have that knowledge, too. We're all just one. I don't get the sense that we're separate entities over there… we stay there, in the collective knowledge, until we're ready to come back to learn more, to receive more information."

Others experience a more solitary aspect. After that difficult life in World War II, my own personal NPE encounter was solitary but healing. I found myself on a perfect porch overlooking a perfect garden on a perfect spring day. That is where I processed the life I just left, with an occasional attempt of comfort from a helpful guide. But my trauma from that life did not switch off instantly. I cringed when I *ran* that personality, refusing connection with my guides; I was just too wounded.

When I finally asked my guide, "Why am I all alone?" my guide replied, "You're not!" And with those words, it was as if this world of the garden fell away and I was surrounded by loving energies. Only then did I experience "The Unity" my client described, where I became a point of light. Like a cloud in the sky, which is actually composed of countless drops of water, I became aware of what I thought was a "cloud" consisting of an infinite number of other individual lights. (Note that my NPE was still in the somewhat "physical" garden environment until I let go and became non-physical.)

Upon mentioning that a life seemed difficult, one participant corrected me, "Difficulty is relative to our limited physical perspective…it's only a challenge in this life…it's not like we can really make a right or wrong decision…it's the *experience* of it…there are no wrong decisions, but you *can* make better decisions." As for making choices, "A or B, you're going to learn either way." There is no judging because, "it's impossible not to learn." Their words might be too long for a tattoo, but the wisdom is profound: *There are no wrong decisions—you're going to learn either way. It's impossible not to learn.*

In what is possibly my favorite exchange to date, another client changed my use of the phrase "the other side" in describing the NPE state upon transitioning out of a physical body: "The 'other side'? I don't think that's a good description. To me the 'other side' implies that this (the physical) is the main side. *It's actually the opposite.*"

Applying my favorite two-word phrase, "what if":

> What if what we experience as the physical world
> is actually "the other side," and the Non-Physical
> Experience, this continuity of consciousness Between
> lives, is actually our true home, where we've spent
> most of our time since our release from spirit/source?

Another amazing client response to their NPE: "It felt good to get back to my real body." The word "home" also gets used often. I've lost count how many times I've heard, "It's good to be home."

I've applied some of this wisdom to the challenges I face in my daily life. Accessing and navigating the Non-Physical Experience Between lives is the richest acknowledgment that we truly are spiritual beings having a human experience.

> *Looking to our past will show us our future, as we ourselves will one day be someone else's former life. What we are learning in these therapies about the fate of our former lives, therefore, is instructing us in our fate as well.*
>
> Christopher Bache, *Lifecycles* [xxix]

RUNNING TIP:
NAMES AS PLACEHOLDERS

I use names or titles when I type up my notes after a session, such as the "Bedouin Mailman," the "Jongleur," the "Aztec Priest," "George." This is my attempt to capture the essence of that Other life personality without defining them in linear Time. It's more of a poetic labeling than a historical designation.

I am not at all interested in finding the gravestones or birth/death records of any of my Past lives; I leave that to other practitioners. My goal is to access the deeper emotional history of these Past life personalities. And it's also an exercise in trusting your first impression; capturing that first perception becomes important. Some of these placeholder names persist, others change with further exploration.

As (Benjamin) Franklin put it in an epitaph he drafted as a young man:

> *"The Body of B. Franklin,*
> *Printer;*
> *Like the cover of an old Book,*
> *Its Contents torn out,*
> *And stripped of its Lettering and Gilding,*
> *Lies here, Food for Worms.*
> *But the Work shall not be wholly lost:*
> *For it will, as he believed, appear once more*

In a new and more perfect Edition,
Corrected and amended
By the Author."

Allen Craig Houston, *Benjamin Franklin and the Politics of Improvement*[xxx]

PART 2:
THE HEART OF
THE MATTER

*In which my Past Life Journeying evolves
from the cerebral to the emotional.*

*"It's really extraordinary that something that for so long
was considered sort of peripheral to our lives — feeling
— is in fact the very beginning, the foundation, the inau-
gural event of what becomes consciousness," said Antonio
Damasio, an international leader in neuroscience who runs
the (USC Brain and Creativity) institute with his wife, Hanna
Damasio, an expert in brain imaging...In his acclaimed
book* Descartes' Error, *he challenges French philosopher
René Descartes' famous saying, "I think, therefore I am."
It's more like I feel, therefore I am.*

- Jean Guerrero, in his *Los Angeles Times* column[xxxi]

OTHER PRACTITIONERS WORKING WITHOUT HYPNOSIS: MORRIS NETHERTON & ROGER WOOLGER

"Even if past lives do exist, what does that mean to my life today? That was then and this is now." To answer this, I once again use the nine months of pregnancy as an example. During each month of pregnancy, the fetus physically develops what the preceding month makes possible. Each stage of its growth and development uses the prior stage as a foundation upon which to build until viability is reached. It is much the same with the soul's evolutionary process as each lifetime builds and expands upon the experiences of those preceding it. This current life experience is a reflection of a stage of growth and development your soul has achieved thus far. Past lives, therefore, are important because they constitute the basis of our identity (and they hold the key to resolving what needs to be completed to move towards the next stage in one's development).

Morris Netherton, Past Life Therapist[xxxii]

In 2016, I organized the Asheville Past Lives Project Meetup. For the first year of our monthly gatherings, I took the opportunity to explain what the Awareness Technique was and how to use it, since almost no one knew about it. I also was able to hear people share their Past life experiences.

After a year of monthly meetings, it became obvious that I needed to offer something more to keep the momentum going: the daunting prospect of leading an entire group into a Past life journey. I had no idea how to do this—everyone else who did work with groups was using a standard hypnotic regression technique…a progressive relaxation of the body followed by directions to move down a staircase, usually entering a garden or sacred space where the instructions were given to access a room or location for the Past life exploration. (I've always been intrigued by the way hypnotic regressions proceed by moving down and going deeper, while the Awareness Technique moves *up* and out of the body before coming down into the Past life.)

After decades of work, on my own and with others using the Swygards' Awareness Technique with its non-hypnotic induction, I wasn't drawn to changing course or getting certified in hypnosis. As I've written previously, I was part of that population who felt I couldn't be easily or effectively hypnotized, despite working with multiple advanced practitioners. Plus, my goal was to find and implement the *next* step forward in Past life exploration, something that was faster, easier, and more immediate for more people.

So, I kept asking myself and my higher self: what *is* the next step forward in exploring Past lives? (Arrogant? A little, but hey, I am a Leo. And I've survived both the music and film businesses on both coasts.) I spent a year researching other Past life practitioners who worked without hypnosis. This led me to the work of two incredible but underappreciated practitioners: Morris Netherton and Roger Woolger.

From his offices in Beverly Hills, California, Morris Netherton, Ph.D. practiced what he described as the Past Life Therapy Center De-Hypnosis Method for 45 years. He wasn't shy about expressing his opinions: *PLTC utilizes a focused state of de-hypnosis, unlike hypnosis that often entails suggestive methods, which rarely works long-term, if at all.*[xxxiii]

A man after my own non-hypnotic-induction heart! There is great wisdom in his ideas. According to Hans TenDam, author of the excellent 2012 book *Exploring Reincarnation*:

> *Netherton uses "postulates"—ingrained programs, vows, promises, ingrown attitudes, verbally fixed in the mind and sometimes repressed—as triggers for past life recall. When we describe our problems or fears, these postulates come up as repetitive statements. The point is to pick out these ritual formulas, preferably giving them an expressive character. For example, "I've got to get out of this!" or "Nobody likes me!" or "I don't need anybody." Repeating, or having us repeat these key sentences a few times, elicits their suppressed emotional charge and focuses us. Directly following this, we are asked to picture ourselves in a situation in which this sentence is literally true or actually spoken, with all its corresponding emotions.*[xxxiv]

Netherton would conduct a two-hour intake with a new client, copying down the type of statements referenced above, and then say, "You're already there, take me with you," moving directly into a Past life session. I've had great success with this approach with my own clients, such that after only a five- or ten-minute conversation I could uncover the issue from a Past life that was rising to the surface of their consciousness. (I called it my "Spidey-sense" that was triggered when I heard the phrase, topic, or emotion needing to be explored.) The emphasis on emotions in Netherton's work, which I often use with my one-on-one clients, led me to Roger Woolger.

Roger Woolger's influential 1987 book *Other Lives, Other Selves* was subtitled *A Jungian Psychotherapist Discovers Past Lives*. My favorite quote from the book bridges pioneering psychotherapist Carl Jung and a Past-lives approach:

> *"A complex arises where we have experienced a defeat in life," according to Carl Jung. I believe we need to expand Jung's dictum to the extent of stating that a complex arises where we have experienced a defeat in any life…(v)ery often an illness may conceal an old "defeat in life" in symbolic language.*[xxxv]

The deeper I dug into Woolger's work, the more I resonated with his approach. He beautifully described something I saw in my clients and in my own work, what I refer to as "echoes" exerting an influence from another life:

> *Each of us carries within us a whole other world, shadowy and fantastic, to be sure, but teemingly alive with inner figures, melodramas, grievances, and fears, that are constantly exerting their influence over our every word and deed.*[xxxvi]

I credit Woolger's *Other Lives, Other Selves*—along with the Sounds True audio version—with enlightening me to the concept that a powerful emotion can be the bridge into a Past life exploration, and that this could be the method to guide a group into a Past life. The exercises in the audio version of the book were incredibly effective and used no induction; they simply followed an emotion. But when putting this into practice, I noticed something interesting—the emotions were wired in both directions! We could follow them from the Present life back into the Past, as Netherton suggested, *or* allow a powerful emotion in a Past life to draw us back to it, to experience it again and uncover why it was "echoing" into our Present life.

GUIDING GROUP PAST LIFE JOURNEYS

I intuitively felt Woolger's method was the best way to guide a group into a Past life experience, but I knew that when I guided a client into a Past life journey, very often the first emotion that wanted to be acknowledged and released was a trauma or deeply felt emotion, often expressed with tears. I credit Akashic Records practitioner and coach Rev. Sandra Gelinas with reminding me, in a conversation at a networking event, that not all Past lives have to be traumatic and that we can also tap into positive emotions from Past experiences.

With Sandra's idea in mind, I devised the following guidance to invite all members of the Asheville Meetup group to reconnect to an experience in a previous existence that was so happy, so joyful, and so positive that it attracts them back to that Past life body and personality, allowing us to access that person's happiness. This was my guidance to the group:

> Open yourself to the possibility that somewhere on this planet, in a different body, in a different place and time, you experienced a lifetime or an event that was so positive and so happy—in whatever way you define happiness—that those powerful positive emotions will guide you back to that Previous personality, back to that Previous body, back to that place and time on the planet, to experience that positivity once again.

Imagine yourself roaming around this planet—a big blue marble beneath you—and feel the places on the planet where you experienced these positive emotions. There may be more than one location drawing you down to the planet...but follow the most powerful emotion down to the earth, and firmly but gently bring your feet to stand on the ground and inhabit this Past life body.

Take a minute to orient yourself in this body. Feel your feet on the ground and determine whether you are indoors or out, whether it is day or nighttime. And then look down at your feet and determine what, if anything, is covering your feet.

Become aware what, if anything, is covering the lower part of your body and then the upper part of your body. Is this a male or female body? Become aware of your hair. Ask or feel if anything is covering your head. Become aware of the age range of this body: Is it a child's body? An adolescent? An adult? Middle-aged? Or an elder?

When you feel connected to this Past life personality, expand your awareness to your surroundings. Are you alone? Are there other people there? Any animals? Are you carrying anything with you: any bags, any tools, or any weapons? Spend some time connecting to this Past life personality, and then feel into their heart. Ask, "What is the source of this joy, this happiness?" Is it something they possess? Is it an object? Is it the location, or just being in a natural setting? Is it connected to a person, a relationship, or to a group of people? Or is it what they are doing that brings them great joy?

Reconnect to this emotion. This is your experience, your history that you've recovered. Now feel it in your Present-day body. Spend some time marinating in this happiness.

Then ask yourself: Is this happiness in my life now? Have I experienced this positivity earlier in my life? How did it go away? Is this something I can work towards having more of in my life?

Connect to that Past life joy and feel it in your heart now. Recover that positive experience and bring it back into your life today. Then feel the chair supporting you. Feel the clothes on your body and the air in this room. Take as long as you need to, but welcome back. You can open your eyes whenever you are ready.

Since I won't take a client anywhere that I haven't first explored, I did this on my own...and you can, too! Have someone read this to you as you follow along. Or record the script it into your phone and let your own voice guide you. Try it and let me know how this works for you by emailing me at timelinejourneying@gmail.com.

Here are my notes from my first "Following a Positive Emotion" session:

The Indian Mother: I am barefoot, standing on sandy dirt. But I can't see my feet easily because I am so very pregnant. I am a young mother in modest circumstances, wearing a simple, sari-type covering. Long dark hair pulled back, no jewelry or rings. Standing outside a small hut, mud covering straw, we are neither rich nor poor, but comfortable. My husband is off working. I feel not only the warmth of our relationship, but the overriding emotion of LOVE for this child, due very soon. Then I access the joyous experience of holding my newborn, a boy. I know his name and the love is now being expressed in my caring for him.

As a man of a certain age with no children, this is not an experience that I've had. Nor will I ever know the feeling of carrying a child (not in this body, in this life) but it was a profound experience. (By the way, I strongly advocate everyone take the opportunity to experience a life in a body of the opposite sex. I predict that your relationships will be changed if you allow yourself to know the other side of the romantic, familial, or business equation.)

The group sharing that I encourage is my favorite part of this process. Participants are often surprised to discover a "group effect" with common themes or locations being reported. My most significant takeaway from dozens of group-based Past life journeys? No one *ever* mentioned wealth or fame as a source of Past life soul happiness that was powerful enough to draw them back to experience it again.

Later—and sometimes opening it to suggestions from the members of the group—I expanded to use the awareness of other powerful emotions like, "What was your most spiritually advanced lifetime?" or, "What was your most powerful lifetime, however you define power?" Or even as suggested by a workshop participant, "Who are these animals in your Present life, these 'furry family members'? Have you had a relationship with them in another life, and what form did it inhabit in that life?"

Having participants connect with their love for their pets and follow that emotion back into a shared Past life was interesting and sometimes surprising. Sometimes they were in the form of a completely different animal—dogs, cats, and birds appeared in their Present form, as horses, and even as a wolf!

Roger Woolger brilliantly refers to this as "experiential exploration." This was the breakthrough that allowed me to conduct group sessions at my Meetup groups, workshops, and presentations. It was also Woolger who alerted me to Shadow Work, the next aspect I would be exploring.

Next up: my rediscovery of another pioneer in group exploration— Dick Sutphen—who took a very different approach.

Once we begin to explore a whole series of past lives, a very prominent feature stands out: there is a constant process of reversal from one kind of personality to its opposite.

Roger Woolger, *Other Lives, Other Selves* [xxxvii]

DICK SUTPHEN AND SHADOW WORK: BOTH VICTIM AND PERPETRATOR

Naturally there will be painful, even shameful aspects of the self that may have to be faced. In Jung's perspective this is what is called shadow *work—looking at unpleasant and often negative characteristics and not repressing them further.*

Roger Woolger, *Other Lives, Other Selves*[xxxviii]

Imagine this scene: it is the mid-1980s and in a Past-lives seminar Dick Sutphen is taking a room full of people into their personal dark night of the soul. In public. In a group.

Imagine the weeping and gnashing of teeth. Sutphen called this work "Bushido" and jokes in one of his books, "*I wish you a miserable past-life regression.*"[xxxix] Not what you'd expect from one of the original New Age personalities who helped put Sedona on the map and authored one of the earliest mass market books on reincarnation with his 1978 *You Were Born to Be Together*. His reasoning is as follows:

> *If your regression experience is vivid and real enough for you to get upset, then I guarantee you this past-life incident is still in your present life. It is programming that is still under the surface, festering and manifesting as problems. By getting in touch with the cause*

in regression, you can totally experience it, possibly resolving your problem...Everything you feel, every attitude, hang-up, fear, and phobia is rooted in your past. There is a past event or series of events that is causing you to experience the present undesirable effect.[xl]

That sums up Sutphen's philosophy and methodology better than I could. Sutphen is an advocate of the belief that "you create everything, that you are totally responsible for everything that happens to you." Luckily, he also stresses that "wisdom erases karma."

Can you make it all right with yourself to release and rise above the past, the past of being a victim and the past of being the bad guy? Can you let go of all the past situations you've lived and suffered? If you are ready to truly forgive yourself, you can release all the undesirable effects right now. You can wipe the slate clean and move forward into your present life clear, focused, in balance and harmony. The choice is yours.[xli]

I do not know many people willing to do this work, exploring Past personalities as both victim and perpetrator, but I knew I had to explore it for myself before I could bring this concept to my clients. Undertaking this work, and then explaining it, is akin to that part of writing described by columnist Red Smith as when *"you simply sit down at the typewriter, open your veins, and bleed."*[xlii] (Trigger warning: some of the following material may be too brutal for sensitive people. In that case, skip to the next chapter.)

Here are my notes from the first part of this process—my ultimate victimization:

My immediate Previous life (in linear Time) was brief and brutal. I was not yet a teenager when war broke out in Europe. As someone who was half-Jewish, any semblance of a normal life was lost when my mother and I were rounded up, loaded into railroad cars like cattle, and relocated to a concentration camp. There I was, separated from my mother and enduring horror as powerful people driven by hate attempted to wipe out huge swaths of the "unwanteds" from the population.

Hunger, cold, and brutality were my daily life. When the pain of daily torment became too much, I snuck out of the sleeping area in an act of defiance and made my way towards the fence, knowing this would draw the attention of the guards and their weapons. I died in a hail of bullets thinking, "What kind of monsters do this to people?"

This was a personal realization of how "time of death" emotions imprint on our energy fields. Now, millions of people on both sides of the conflict died in this second world war, so my case is not unique. But the occasional, lesser cruelties of my Present life triggered my angst. It was only when exposed to Dick Sutphen's work that I summoned the courage to ask a question at the dark heart of this work (with gratitude to Past life practitioner George Duisman for his contribution here). That question: If my Previous life was living out the role of the ultimate victim, does that mean this could have been triggered by a life where I was the ultimate perpetrator?

The Awareness Technique is driven by questions, so it must have been my continual asking, "What kind of monsters do this to people?" that allowed me to open the door to my own inner monster. My answer came as I explored a Past life in medieval times I call "The Court Confessor":

In the medieval period, I was a very large male soldier of great strength who was not deemed sufficiently bloodthirsty. Though my physical size made me ideal to be a warrior, I apparently did not grasp the need to kill all the women and children after vanquishing our enemies. It was thought that a season in the dungeon would toughen me up and improve my utility as a soldier. There, my duties included torturing confessions out of people. Obviously, this was traumatic. But I repressed or adapted in order to survive. The only relief I felt was in drink, and I died alone, overwhelmed by all the deaths I'd caused.

Here is where the concept of the "banality of evil" becomes evident: it was a job, an assignment. It's a cognitive shift to see someone committing heinous acts—someone I would later see as a monster—and imagine them punching the clock for their job, counting the hours until work was done, when they could retire to the pub or wherever. But it literally knocked my legs out from under me to see *myself* committing acts of cruelty...cruelty I would endure myself centuries later, when other misguided patriots—also probably following orders—enslaved and murdered millions because they were "the other."

Then there was the Time factor. This was another awareness of non-linear Time, seeing how a lifetime in the Middle Ages found its counterpart in the mid-1900s instead of the next consecutive life.

I accessed another life where the cruelty was less obvious, but where the political and social echoes remained. I had previously *run* a life as an "Aztec Priest" (once again, this is my descriptive name used to identify a Past life personality, not an attempt at historical accuracy):

> One of my "jobs" (once again, punching the clock!) was to perform a ceremony that the hierarchy believed guaranteed a fruitful harvest and the rain that made it possible. This involved sacrificing a slave during a full moon, removing their heart, and offering it to

the gods, after which it was enclosed in a container stored in a cave.

This priest's knowledge of herbs and potions was on display in two ways: I knew how to sedate the innocent victim so they would not be tortured, and I knew how to sedate myself so that I was in a suitably altered state when performing this ritual. (My Present-day self is aware of the vitamins, herbs, and teas that fill my counters…possibly an echo of this expertise?)

I had the guards do the dirty work of opening the victim's chest cavity so I could access and remove the heart. This was a high ceremony in a consciousness-altering environment complete with torches, incense, and hallucinogens. But underneath this was also the awareness that this was a circus, a spectacle to please the masses and the higher-ups. I knew in my heart that I was a showman, that I had no control over the crops or the weather. I also knew that someday bad weather and a failing crop would see *me* become the sacrifice, and it would be my heart added to the collection when I experienced this death. It was also in *running* this life that I saw a staggering image: a cave of hundreds of containers filled with sacrificed hearts representing decades, and possibly centuries, of these ceremonies.

I had to question myself and ask: was this evil, or just misguided spirituality? Is this still playing out into modern times with our wars and genocides? In my research on Roger Woolger, I found this gem:

> *Instead of saying, "I was that slave master, temple prostitute, tribesmen, etc.," we begin to say instead, "I have a slave master, temple prostitute, tribesman within me."* [xliii]

Or this:

> Not just the victim, but the bully and the rapist in all
> of us also are in need of healing and forgiveness.[xliv]

My reframe was not that I *am* that monster; I *had* that monster in me, and that monster is both deserving and in need of healing. (More on forgiveness and healing below.) I have worked on myself with this very intense practice, this Past-lives version of shadow work, being willing to look at those events and choices which led to being "the bad guy."

What is surprising is to find that for all the times I saw myself as the victim, additional digging uncovered a life where I was the perpetrator, sometimes involving the same people! It is extremely powerful (and, according to Sutphen, necessary), but it is not for everybody. I mention this to inform my readers of the possibilities inherent with deep, deep, dives into Other selves.

Here is my personal note on a session dealing with this topic:

> Consider that the person who seems to be the "bad
> guy" is the one delivering the most important lesson
> in that life, and possibly at great personal cost.

Dick Sutphen passed away in 2020. Because he may be more well-known for his book *You Were Born to be Together Again*, and his extensive library of subliminal audio recordings, his contributions to the field of Past life explorations may be overlooked.

Next up, releasing any stuck emotions with the Release Technique and Ho'oponopono.

> *If I were a mystic, I guess Clarence and my friendship would
> lead me to believe that we…we stood together in other, older
> times. You know, in other lives, along other rivers, in other*

*ancient cities, in other fields, workin' side by side, with the
sun settin' doin' our modest version of God's work.
I'll see you in the next life, Big Man.*

Bruce Springsteen in Netflix's *Springsteen on Broadway*, intuiting a Past life experience when delivering a moving tribute to long-time band member and saxophonist Clarence Clemons.[xlv]

HEALING WITH THE RELEASE TECHNIQUE AND HO'OPONOPONO

In my sessions, I observe that emotional upheaval often occurs when encountering a *significant personality*—a person who has a difficult or momentous influence in a Past life session. When a significant personality is involved in an Other life, you can feel into the energy of that person (or, if you're the fortunate visual type, look into their eyes) and ask, "Does this person resonate with anyone I know or have known in my Present life, even if they appear as a different age, sex, or in a different role?" Seeing the same person, or someone playing that same role, in your Present life can illuminate the presenting issue and provide priceless perspective on that relationship.

I expanded the healing potential of Past Life Journeying with the use of other modalities to clear and release any of these stuck emotions. Two of my favorite clearing methods include the Release Technique, something I've known about since the 1970s, and "Ho'oponopono." I've used these in my personal sessions with great success.

First, the Release Technique: This was one of the first methods that I felt moved a significant amount of energy around an issue. I don't know the source of it, and the internet is not very helpful in clearing this up; maybe telling people about my version of it will stir some recollections. The phrasing (as I learned it) is dated and a bit clumsy, but effective when encountering a significant personality in a Past-lives journey. When you encounter this situation, I suggest you connect to the emotions this personality brings to the surface and address them as if they were sitting across from you:

> I release you. I loose you and let you go.
> I have no reason to hurt you, and you have no reason
> to hurt me.
> That incident that was between us is over.
> You are free and I am free and all is well again
> between us.

The use of the phrase "loose you" always felt odd—maybe a bit Victorian—implying or making the phrase appear to be more ancient than it might be. My research on the Release Technique brought me once again to Dolores Cannon. I've become a fan after spending time listening to her interviews and reading her work. Often when I've disagreed with her opinions on something, further experience led me to realize the wisdom of her work.

From the mid-1980s to her death in 2014, Cannon followed her hypnosis practice into some incredibly strange and interesting places. In a 2010 interview with Regina Meredith (available on Gaia TV and, interestingly, the only interview with Cannon herself in the morass of zero-discernment material on Gaia.com), I heard her describe the importance of clearing our old Karma. Cannon refers to this as "tearing up the contract." Here is the wording she uses:

> *We tried. We really tried. It didn't work. Let's tear up*
> *the contract.*
> *I forgive you; I release you; I let you go.*
> *You go your way with love, I'll go mine.*
> *We don't have to be connected anymore at all.*[xlvi]

This hits the same notes as the wording of Release Technique, and I suspect she may have encountered the same source material as I did back in the day. I recommend adding this to your toolkit. I have been using this "tearing up the contract" to close out my sessions when it's appropriate, along with Ho'oponopono.

Second, Ho'oponopono: The group process of Ho'oponopono morphed outside of Hawaii and addresses how one person's issue becomes the community's issue. The community *"makes a decision to not move on until a point of mutual understanding had been reached."*[xlvii] I don't make any claims to the traditional Hawaiian group healing format of Ho'oponopono, from which this is borrowed. The simplified (and Westernized) four-step process, which combines forgiveness and gratitude, is something I've used to close my sessions as needed, or when emotional upheaval has been experienced. Especially if you've found yourself to be "the bad guy," addressing a significant personality from that Past life, say:

> I'm sorry.
> Please forgive me.
> Thank you.
> I love you. (Or, if that is too difficult, substitute "I send you love.")

I appreciate the difference in these two methods. Ho'oponopono asks for forgiveness and expresses gratitude—the two vital components of healing. One or both can be applied to every situation. (And I always include a statement of gratitude when my higher consciousness has trusted me with the information I received in a session.) The Release Technique takes a contrasting approach: acknowledging the ties that bind, then declaring an end to the cosmic back-and-forth. It sets an intention that both parties are free to move forward with no ill will.

I have found these internal, emotional processes to be much more effective than waving a selenite wand or having someone else declaring the cords cut. I suggest adding these closing rituals to your practice. Let me know how it works for you by emailing me at timelinejourneying@ gmail.com.

Please don't let the term "past lives" mislead you into thinking you've arrived this time around as a separate person from who you've been before, alive, then dead, then alive again. No, what you're living right now is simply the current phase of one life, the same eternal life your spirit has been living and will go on living forever...The more we understand about our past lives, the more sense our current lives make.

Sylvia Browne, *Past Lives, Future Healing* [xlviii]

SHAMANIC JOURNEYS
AND PSYCHONAUTS

At this stage of the Past Lives Project, I was regularly conducting group-based Past life journeys in my meetups and workshops. I was practicing what I believed to be a unique, non-hypnotic method for clients to access Past and Between lives utilizing a hybrid of the Awareness Technique with the addition of the emotion-based approaches of Woolger and Netherton. And, when clients were open to it, diving deeply into how often we "play a role" on both sides of an interaction, experiencing both victim and perpetrator roles.

My next leap into the unknown came when I discovered a weekly shamanic journeying circle in Asheville led by shamanic arts practitioner Gail Gulick and her drumming partner, Dean Buckley of <u>DreamtimeJourneys. net</u>. I went to ask Gail a question and stayed for both of the 20-minute journeys they conduct weekly. To my complete surprise, I received an answer from the journey and the guide whom I encountered…an answer that was so surprising in its point of view that I returned and attended the group for the next few years. Six months into the weekly sessions, I purchased my own single-headed "buffalo" drum and became the drummer for the next few years, which also satisfied my drumming fix.

This shamanic journeying process became another influence on my work, for which I am grateful. I borrowed Gail's two most important steps, which I continue to use in my practice:

1. TRUST THE FIRST IMAGE

In shamanic journeying, this involves putting oneself into an environment where you intend to encounter a spirit animal. Ask it, "Are you my spirit guide?" (From my notes: If you are drawn to multiple guides, pick one and stick with it.) Sometimes these are real-world creatures; my favorites were the monkeys I encountered. (Actually, they looked and acted more like chimpanzees, but "monkey" seemed more appropriate since I approach all names and titles as place holders.) But if you encounter a more fantastical creature, trust the image and follow through with it to grant you access to this non-physical reality.

In Past lives work, this is important since the first image usually appears in response to my question, "Look down and tell me, what, if anything, are you wearing on your feet?" If you are male and see tiny feet in ballet slippers, or are a female encountering large combat boots, trust this image and answer this question honestly. Don't allow your rational mind to convince you that you're making this up, nor give into the fear that it can't be real. Getting past this first step is crucial, and I credit Gail with providing awareness around this.

2. YOU HAVE TO PROMISE TO COME BACK

This always gets a laugh, but it serves notice that we are journeying to a different realm and need to fully return to ordinary consciousness to process our experience. If it weren't delivered so lovingly, the prompt might be, "Promise to come *all the way back*" to ordinary reality so that you can make your way home safely. Bring your experience back to refer to your Present life for the very important critical assessment component.

While I have never had a client or group participant not come fully back, I do recognize the expression of someone who has had their "mind blown," as the hippies used to say. A deep dive can occur in the first session, and it can take a few minutes to return to ordinary reality from this liminal state.

My closing instructions include, "Now reconnect with your physical body in the chair. Feel the chair holding you up. Feel the clothes on your body. Feel the air in the room. Take as long as you need to, but whenever you're ready, open your eyes, and welcome back." Reminding yourself, "That was then, this is now," is another way to fully inhabit our Present-day personality.

What surprised me was how other-worldly my shamanic experiences were in the group, as were those I heard from other journeyers in the time we spent sharing afterwards, especially from the newbies. (I always do this in my groups. While I tell people that sharing is optional, it is my favorite part of the process.) What I heard was often so extraordinary, the only explanation I can think of for describing it is: "psychedelic without the drugs and only lasting 20 minutes."

This got me thinking about how someone who pursues psychedelics for consciousness expansion might appreciate the Past Life Journeying experience. In reading an article by Michael Pollan in the *Wall Street Journal*, one quotation jumped out at me:

> *...a mystical experience can permanently shift a person's perspective and priorities.*[xlix]

Pollan's book *How to Change Your Mind* examines the work of researchers using state-of-the-art technology to study what happens in the brain under the influence of psychedelics. One of his surprise discoveries is how the psychedelic brain matches up with the brains of experienced meditators. I wonder how the brain of someone on a Past Lives Journey would appear on an fMRI. Even more so, what the brain scan looks like of someone exploring the Non-Physical Experience (NPE) Between lives—where consciousness is navigating while untethered to a physical body.

Pollan's book refers to the person experiencing psychedelics as a "psychonaut"—someone who uses psychedelics for consciousness expansion. He had this deep observation:

> *If it were possible to temporarily experience another person's mental state, my guess is that it would feel more like a psychedelic state than a "normal" state, because of its massive disparity with whatever mental state is habitual with you.*[1]

A very trippy thought because, in the context of Past and Future lives exploration, experiencing what seems like another personality's mental (and emotional) state is only the starting point. Some of the best Other life journeys can be likened to mystical experiences because we have set our conscious intention to temporarily experience a different mental state, with the added layer of knowing that we are the person inhabiting that mental state, aware of their back story and justifications for their behaviors.

Like the psychonaut's inner adventure, the Past life journey requires some unpacking afterwards. There is the mental disparity between our Present- and Other-life selves (especially when the Previous incarnation making those decisions acts in a way that is evil, like a jerk, or both), combined with the resonance from that Past life state that is echoing into our Present life. That "echoing" is the reason we are drawn to examine that Other life. Here is Pollan's take on this:

> *The long-term fate of the novel connections formed during the psychedelic experience, whether they prove durable or evanescent, might depend on whether we recall and, in effect, exercise them after the experience ends. (This could be as simple as recollecting what we experienced, reinforcing it during the integration process, or using meditation to reenact the altered state of consciousness.) Franz Vollenweider has suggested*

that the psychedelic experience may facilitate neuro-plasticity.[li]

Neuroplasticity is the ability of the brain to grow and reorganize itself, especially in response to learning or new experiences. I believe that all these aspects also apply to Past Life Journeying, though I never considered advertising it from the standpoint of "facilitating neuroplasticity."

In his 2019 book *LSD and the Mind of the Universe* (beautifully subtitled *Diamonds from Heaven*), Christopher Bache courageously narrates 73 psychedelic journeys over a 20-year period. He undertook these "not as a clinician but as a philosopher," utilizing Stanislav Grof's therapeutic model as a foundation. Bache describes his "philosophical method" in three steps:

1. *to systematically push the boundaries of experience in carefully structured psychedelic sessions*

2. *to make a complete and accurate record of experiences immediately following each session, and*

3. *to critically analyze your experience, bringing it into dialogue with other fields of knowledge and with the experiences of other psychedelic explorers*

   By moving systematically back and forth between psychedelically amplified states of consciousness and our ordinary consciousness, where these experiences can be digested and evaluated, philosophical discourse is expanded and deepened.[lii]

I was gratified when reading the above to realize that I had instinctively been using Bache's "philosophical method" in my personal sessions.

- intending to push the accepted boundaries with a non-hypnotic means of accessing Past, Between, and—eventually—Future lives

- recording audio of the sessions, which I then transcribe and utilize for details I might have missed while in the depths of the experience

- critically assessing the material by revisiting it before undertaking another session, putting it in context with my previous sessions and the work of other researchers and practitioners

- accessing an Other life without hypnosis and enabling the client to evaluate the Other life experience (and the significant personalities in that life) using the current incarnation as a reference point

(And in an interesting sync, Christopher Bache has also written about Past Lives; I've quoted from his 1994 book *Lifecycles: Reincarnation and the Web of Life*.)

After particularly intense Past life journeys, I have often thought (and heard brave participants say), "Wow, what a trip!" My concept of the shamanic or Past/Future life exploration as a "trip" has been altered after reading these books. But—and this is significant—I am not advocating psychedelics as a consciousness-expanding device. In fact, Pollan's book of research into psychedelics has reaffirmed my belief in the power of Past- and Between lives exploration for the purpose of expanding consciousness. With this powerful tool we have the ability to inhabit, with full consciousness, the mental and physical state of a different race, culture, environment, and—for the ultimate contrast to our Present life—a different sex. That's a journey that can shift a person's perspective and priorities!

For more on the non-drug psychedelic experience, I advocate shamanic journeying with a trusted guide. Shamanic excursions influenced my inner work dramatically, to the point where I was inspired to christen my own work as "Past Life Journeying."

For an even deeper dive, connect with me for a personal Past Life Journey outside of linear Time and obtain a different perspective on the multitude of timelines that your soul contains.

The years when I was pursuing my inner images were the most important in my life—in them everything essential was decided. It all began then; the later details are only supplements and clarifications of the material that burst forth from the unconscious, and at first swamped me. It was the prima materia for a lifetime's work.

Swiss psychiatrist Carl Jung, *Memories, Dreams, Reflections*[liii]

RUNNING TIP: DISCERNMENT

One of my favorite quotations, and some of the best advice I encountered doing this work, was from hypnotherapist and author Mary Lee LaBay:

Just because you're dead doesn't mean you're smart.[liv]

LaBay was referring to our very human desire to ascribe omniscience to "discarnate entities," or what the Soul Phone Foundation refers to as "post-material collaborators" (the deceased). It addresses our assumption that enlightenment comes immediately upon leaving the body. LaBay reminds us that:

You do not suddenly gain a body of wisdom or knowledge that was not part of your consciousness before death. After death, psychic vision is only slightly clearer.[lv]

Bravo, Mary! The whole concept of discernment in these matters is best described by this quote attributed to everyone from Carl Sagan to Richard Dawkins (but actually belonging to Walter Kotschnig):

Let us keep our minds open, by all means...but don't keep your minds so open that your brains fall out.[lvi]

Mary Lee LaBay again:

People also mistakenly assumed that because their spirit guide is in the astral, he or she is omniscient, has perfect vision and wisdom. In truth, it doesn't work that way at all.[lvii]

In my take on this, I extend that advice outward into the galaxy:

Just because you're from the Pleiades star system, or the Galactic Council, or Atlantis, doesn't mean you're smart.

If we truly want to advance our awareness, I propose that it is our duty to look behind the curtain at the wizards giving us directions, and from an Other-lives perspective, examine our relationship to these consciousnesses. Although this might make it sound like I am still skeptical about channeling, consider this advice: I treat channeled information like I treat every bit of information on the internet—as an opinion and not a fact—until proven otherwise. (The discarnate entity known as "James," who you'll meet later, is my example of a source whose "opinion" I have come to treasure.)

I suggest inquiring into these discarnate entities in a Past Life Journeying session by asking, "Who are these consciousnesses and why are they talking through me? What is my relation to them, if any?"

And always, always check for unfinished business being played out in detail in our Present timeline. How? By asking, "Does this source of wisdom resonate with anyone I know, or have known, in my Present life or any Other lives I've explored?"

Experience has taught me that significant personalities tend to return throughout our incarnations. One interesting area of investigation is asking whether these significant personalities can recur when they're not inhabiting a physical body.

There's no line at the bank for being ahead of your time.

Comedian/Actor/Filmmaker Albert Brooks, quoted in Judd Apatow's
Sick in the Head – Conversations About Life and Comedy[lviii]

PART 3:
IT'S ABOUT TIME!

*In which I "doubt my doubts" about
the possibility of Future lives.*

*I find my earliest memories covering the anachronistic fea-
tures of a previous incarnation. Clear recollections came
to me of a distant life in which I had been a yogi amid the
Himalayan snows. These glimpses of the past, by some dimen-
sionless link, also afforded me a glimpse of the future.*

Paramahansa Yogananda, *Autobiography of a Yogi*[lix]

DR. BRUCE GOLDBERG: NON-LINEAR TIME, SIMULTANEOUS AND FUTURE LIVES

To discover that our life is connected to a series of lives does not reduce the value of this current life... To realize that our present life is only one cycle in the life of a being whose limits we cannot envision in no way diminishes the immediate self we now are. Like the chambered nautilus, one side cannot exist without the other. We are not rendered insignificant by this larger being but integral to it...Everything that has passed before leads up to us, and we are creating the future.

Christopher M. Bache, *Lifecycles: Reincarnation and the Web of Life*[lx]

If you've stayed with me this far, you should know we've been "coloring within the lines," sticking to the tried-and-true methods made familiar by other practitioners in the field. Now let's get weird and dive into what author Michael Talbot calls "deeper depths to plumb."

It wasn't too long ago that I thought I'd never be writing about—or even considering—the information I'm about to share with you. Much like the tinnitus-plagued musician who moved to Asheville and found Page Bryant's beautiful book of channeled information, *The Spiritual Reawakening of the Great Smoky Mountains*, it was the work of Bruce Goldberg, Michael Talbot, Tam Mossman, and Eric Wargo whom I credit with expanding my awareness into areas previously too uncomfortable to explore.

Looking back, it seems the alarm clock for my awakening around the concept of Time rang in February 2020, when I saw Dr. Bruce Goldberg present at the week-long UFO Mega Conference in Laughlin, Nevada. I was previously unimpressed with exploring Future lives, a failing on my part I now acknowledge. But that day, I made a conscious effort to open myself to Goldberg's ideas at his talk "Time Travelers from the Future and the Fifth Dimension." I left the presentation (the 25th I'd attended that week!) impressed but unaware that I had just undergone a transformative experience signaling the beginning of something new.

Once home, I ordered his book, *Past Lives, Future Lives Revealed*, and learned Dr. Goldberg was a dentist who learned hypnosis to help his patients, then found himself doing more hypnosis than dentistry. This then led to conducting Past life regressions using the classic hypnotic process, which led to Future life explorations with the discovery of a "chrononaut"—a time traveler—from *the 35th century when teleportation is mastered for time traveling back and forward through time.*[lxi]

Goldberg describes a session similar to Brian Weiss' introduction to this work: he asked a client to go to the source of an issue and was then surprised and challenged by the result. In Weiss' case, the client went back to 1800 BC (inspiring his first book *Many Lives, Many Masters)*. In Goldberg's case, the client went *forward* to the 23rd century. This led to his first book, 1988's *Past Lives, Future Lives*, which he claims was "the first book ever written on Future life progression."

I was willing to go the distance with Goldberg's ideas because of something he wrote in the "The Big Picture" chapter of this book: *Psychic genetics is* [sic] *more important than biological genetics in determining the character of our lives.*[lxii] I'd always felt this was true and appreciated his acknowledgement of these "psychic genetics," what I called "echoes" from Other lives into our Present circumstances.

But there was nothing else about this Future life information with which I was comfortable. And before seeing Goldberg's presentation, I wouldn't have seriously considered it myself, so if you find yourself feeling hesitant and doubtful when reading this next bit of information, welcome to my world!

After his presentation I opened myself to the possibility of exploring a Future life. (As you'll see later, Goldberg was instrumental in guiding me to "George," my own 29th century incarnation.) But I was only confident with these mini attempts at Time travel as long as we were moving from Past to Present to Future in linear fashion.

> But what if…a new concept of Time begins with releasing the assumption that our lives can only proceed from Past to Present to Future?

I learned how attached I was to linear Time when I had my own personal session with hypnotherapist John Till. During the session I discovered a monk I called "Maleek," one of my most compelling Other lives from my very distant Past. I encountered Maleek after asking my higher self about the origin of my present-day, Past lives work. My notes:

- Stone room, small window, cot, sandals, hooded robe, close-cut hair, late teens/early 20s, a chamber where I do the majority of my work

- A spiritual practice establishing a connection to non-physical spiritual sources, training in private to get my questions answered

- Afterwards, taking notes, but we don't share in a group setting, most of work is done in private and someone is collecting this material

- Material is split between physical, mental, and spiritual-based illness, different categories and different approaches to healing depending on source, which is later collected and compared

- This is someone's larger spiritual project, a group of elders who've been doing this work for multiple generations, finding people who can make the connection and bring forth trustworthy information without having ego involved—there is no feedback or "patting on back," nor doing this for any reason but the work itself

- We're up on a mountain; villagers below know about us and have access to a clinic, but we don't otherwise interact

- I've been doing this since I was 12, when I visited the clinic as a patient

- Not much talking, but chanting is involved, we come down to morning prayer/chanting, meal is silent, tea then return to room, no chores for me at this level, but more/greater workload is expected of me

- I know what an honor it is to be in this "power spot," there are transcendent qualities to this location, being here enables a higher state of awareness, just in it 24/7, energy is supportive, borderline nirvana/higher-state consciousness the whole time, this may be why we don't leave the location

I continued for five sessions—or journeys—to see the entirety of Maleek's life from a 12-year-old hanging around the clinic above his village, to finally being allowed to join the teaching monastery higher up the mountain, to progressing from student to teacher with his/my own classes, and—finally—to working with beings of light even further up the mountain, whose mere presence was transcendent. (When I asked about that location today, I was told that the mountain range we were inhabiting no longer *exists!*) I lived Maleek's experience as he communicated with the consciousness of a non-physical being "in a manner that was very conversational, not the bowing-and-scraping relationship from a cross-legged position, but just like having tea with a familiar person. It's familial...like being with a trusted family member, feeling mutual love and respect."

The events leading up to the end of this life showed me a very old but still-vibrant man who attained a high level of consciousness equal to the light beings who trained him/me. I experienced what it is like to consciously drop the physical body…not because of illness or old age, but because a life's work was complete.

Discovering Maleek turned out to be a turning point in my current work. I assumed that since Maleek was so far in the Past of linear Time, he would be far behind me in progress as well, maybe closer to the origin of my Present-day work. Instead, I had to open myself to the possibility that, in spite of living and working in a pre-industrial culture thousands or even hundreds of thousands of years ago, Maleek achieved a level of spiritual attainment that could be the pinnacle of my multi-lifetime spiritual efforts.

In other words, a millennia ago I had already achieved what I struggle and strive for today. This 21st century spiritual seeker has a Past life where this was his life's work! (*And present-day Bobby congratulated himself on finally finishing something!*)

Good luck wrapping your head around the idea that *a millennia ago* you achieved what you only struggle for today!

This was the vital "clue" I missed, upending my expectations that lives need to proceed in a linear fashion…realizing Maleek progressed further in the distant Past than I have in all of my incarnations since then, including my Present life (so far). I recall being confused about this discrepancy until I read and grasped the ideas Bruce Goldberg presented in *Past Lives, Future Lives Revealed*.

Seeing this non-linear progression in my own Timeline was a personal reckoning for me. With this experience I finally understood that our movement through Time does *not* necessarily proceed in a linear direction—from Past to Present to Future—forcing me to reframe my concept of Time.

I was completely comfortable with exploring Past lives, and even the concept that a combination of awareness, forgiveness, and gratitude could heal our Past life personalities and create results in our Present life. The "Court Confessor" life from a previous chapter was obviously traumatized by his actions on the job. Forgiving him, and the aspect of myself he alerted me to, was necessary to process the lessons from that life.

But for healing to occur there had to be some interaction between my Present and Other lives. This opened the "Time door" further for the next step in my understanding: the concept of *Simultaneous* lives:

> What if...all of our lives—Past, Present, and Future—
> are occurring simultaneously?

This idea was something I'd heard from multiple sources over the years, including way back in the 1970s from the "Seth" books (about the trance entity channeled by writer Jane Roberts). That all of our lives are occurring simultaneously is something Goldberg liberally applied to upend the relationship between cause and effect:

> *...because all time is simultaneous, the cause of a pres-*
> *ent-day problem could very well rest in the future.*[lxiii]

And, as I learned from my life as Maleek, the completion or resolution could be in the distant Past!

By expanding my personal perception to include non-linear and Simultaneous lives, I now have a deeper awareness of Maleek and my Other life personalities—Future *and* Past—possessing talents and abilities that I struggle to achieve in my Present life. The non-hypnotic model allows us to refer to our Present life while *running* a Past life, enabling a two-way connection between Maleek's work and my own in Present day. After five journeys to Maleek's world, I sense how my striving is impacted by Maleek's accomplishments, *and* how my beginner's attempts today further nurture Maleek's work in the Past. The concept of Simultaneous lives explains this ongoing reciprocity between my Present and Other lives.

Here is Goldberg's further elucidation on the concept of Simultaneous Time:

*Modern day physicists use the term space-time con-
tinuum (coined by Albert Einstein) to illustrate the
fact that there is no such thing as the past, present, or
future as we know it. All of our lives are being lived at
the same moment, but at different frequencies. Thus,
your past lives are occurring right now on a different
frequency along with your present and future lives.
They are all affecting each other. You are thus able to
change the past and future by changing the present.*[lxiv]

I found it fascinating that Goldberg wrote about changing the
Present *and* the Future. He described this occurring during a Future-
life progression:

*I asked the patient to go to the origin of a difficulty
and she went forward to the 23rd century! The future
life illustrates a karmic lesson or pattern, which is
usually manifested in their current life. This often
includes the same people and provides a way to learn
from the future to correct the present, thereby affecting the future.*[lxv]

The starting point for a Past life exploration is to heal the "karmic
lessons or patterns" that we uncover in our Previous lives by applying those
tools mentioned earlier: awareness, tearing up the contract, gratitude, and
forgiveness. That release of blocked emotional energy can be experienced
as healing in our current life. Goldberg expands this "energy exchange"
even further: going *forward* to see how our Present energies are projected
into the Future life, then using that potential outcome—and our satisfac-
tion with it—to adjust the Present life, which in turn adjusts our Future.
The circle of life reframed!

I hope readers can see by Maleek's example what becomes possible
with the deeper dives and multiple journeys. (More on this "looping"
between Past, Present, and Future lives when we examine Eric Wargo's

work later.) In the next chapter we'll talk about Michael Talbot's work. He introduced me to a concept that expands upon Simultaneous lives—"Adjacent" lives—to account for the interaction of all of our lives, backwards and forwards.

MICHAEL TALBOT:
PAST LIVES AND TIME IN A
HOLOGRAPHIC UNIVERSE

*The evidence…suggests that we are still children when it comes
to understanding the true nature of time. Unlike all children
placed on the threshold of adulthood, we should put aside
our fears and come to terms with the way the world really is.
For in a holographic universe, or universe in which all things
are just ghostly coruscations* of energy, more than just our
understanding of time must change. There are still other shim-
merings to cross our landscape, still deeper depths to plumb.*

Michael Talbot, *The Holographic Universe*[lxvi]
(*Coruscations are "flashes or sparkles;" I had to look it up.)

T hanks to the "shelf elves," those mystical entities who deliver into my
hands the perfect book with the perfect information at the perfect time,
my next expansion of awareness into the true nature of Time came when
I rediscovered the work of Michael Talbot, author of *The Holographic
Universe*. Talbot was ahead of his time with ideas bridging ancient wisdom and quantum physics and—while I remember reading it not long
after its release in 1991—re-reading it after my deep dive into Past lives
was a revelation.

I can't believe how much of the information I'd been *un*able to grasp
at the time has become accepted, common knowledge. (Someone much

wiser than me pointed out that there are many quantum physicists but no singular Quantum Physics, which is why there are so many competing theories, of which the holographic model is just one.) I had radically reframed my concept of Time, now respectfully spelled with a capital T, beginning with the most basic "what if" question:

> What if Time does not operate the way we thought?
> In re-examining our Past life explorations, can there
> be a new way to conceive of Time?

Talbot investigates these ideas in a section titled "Time Out of Mind" which covers much of the same ground I only recently incorporated into my work, and he wrote it over 30 years ago! In this chapter, he considers the work of Past (and Future) life researchers Helen Wambach, Joel Whitton, and Ian Stevenson, and explained how their work fit into quantum physics (especially theoretical physicist David Bohm's research.) Talbot's theory of the holographic universe considers how seeing the "whole in every part" of the hologram can provide a new model in which to view both physical reality and consciousness:

> *Remember that in a holographic universe, location is*
> *itself an illusion. Just as an image of an apple has no*
> *specific location on a piece of holographic film, in a*
> *universe that is organized holographically things and*
> *objects also possess no definite location; everything*
> *is ultimately non-local, including consciousness.*[lxvii]

That's a very "wooey" spiritual concept crossing over from quantum physics!

It was an even greater surprise to discover Talbot's 1987 *Your Past Lives: A Reincarnation Handbook* (delivered by the shelf elves, and in hardcover no less!) in which he had obviously done a lot of his own Past lives exploration and was one of those lucky enough to remember Previous life incarnations well into childhood. *Your Past Lives* explores a wide variety of techniques including dreaming, self-hypnosis, keeping a

Past lives journal, guided meditations (including the Christos Technique), and his own process called the "Resonance Method" which this quote summarizes beautifully:

Through analysis of your present strong tendencies you can pretty accurately surmise what kind of life you led before.

Paramahansa Yogananda, *Man's Eternal Quest*[lxviii]

Talbot's Resonance Method involves this same category of self-reflection:

One of the easiest ways for you to begin to decipher your past lives is simply to analyze your current psychological makeup. Many past-life researchers believe that past-life origins can be found not only for current emotional and physical problems, moods, habits, talents, and ways of relating with people, but even for food preferences, clothing tastes, nuances of personality, facial expressions, and body language. By determining which of these various pieces of yourself are holdovers from other lives, you can begin to formulate certain pictures of who and what you've been before. This is what the Resonance Method will help you do...As you use the Resonance Method, remember one cardinal rule: No single piece of information means anything. Pieces of information only start to mean something when they fit together into larger pictures.[lxix]

Talbot's book functions as a how-to guide which covers Past life explorations as thoroughly as Page Bryant explored vortexes in her book. And, like Bryant's work of channeled information, it gets weird...uncomfortably weird for me at the time. Talbot devotes a challenging section to "Past-Life Exploration with Trance Entities" and the work of various "discarnate entities," which he describes as: ...*personalities who claim to be human (and other) souls who inhabit non-physical levels of reality beyond our physical dimension.*[lxx]

And with gratitude to Page Bryant, I applied a healthy dose of discernment, but opened my heart and mind to exploring this new source of information from non-physical sources, especially that reference to "human and other souls." Talbot:

> *Although it is obvious that further research is required to determine [the] authenticity of trance information sources, at the very least the pronouncements of discarnate entities provides interesting working hypotheses for some of the greatest mystical questions of all time. However, if discarnate entities turn out to be what they claim, such a discovery would have implications far greater than Columbus' discovery of the New World, or even humankind's first step on the moon. In short, we may be forced to completely re-assess our image of ourselves and our role in the cosmos.*"[lxxi]

As with Page Bryant's work, opening myself to this source of wisdom forced me to re-assess my attitudes and confront my closed-mindedness; it was only the quality of the information that persuaded me of its sageness, and I am grateful to Talbot for prodding me to take the leap off that ledge.

Putting this book into its historical context, *Your Past Lives* was published in 1987 when there was what Talbot described as an "abundance of discarnate entities," a time when J. Z. Knight's "Ramtha" and Jane Roberts' "Seth" books were bestsellers and available through mainstream publishers. He also mentions trance entities with whom I am unfamiliar, such as Jack Purcell's "Lazaris" and Kathryn Ridall's "Diya."

But most impressive to Talbot (and what resonated with my own work) is Tam Mossman's channeling of the discarnate entity he referred to as "James." Interestingly, Mossman was Jane Roberts' editor; he began channeling spontaneously at a dinner party after seven years of watching her go into trance:

> *Mossman's astonished friends asked what the entity would like to be called. On being informed by the entity that it didn't matter what they called it, one of Mossman's friends chose the name "James" at random, and James the entity has been ever since.*[lxxii]

The wisdom about Time *and* Simultaneous lives that "James" brought forth was disruptive to my belief system—in a good way—because it lined up perfectly with similar information I received from my clients and my own personal sessions in this same period. That, plus the recommendation of a trusted source like Michael Talbot, made his "opinion" impossible for me to ignore, especially when it invited me into a new realm of information.

If being uncomfortable is an indication of progress, then I made tremendous progress. As reinforcement to material already received from Goldberg and Talbot himself, I tracked down a copy of Tam Mossman's *Answers from a Grander Self* to read "James'" take on Time:

> *...the answers that discarnate entities give to questions about the mechanics of reincarnation are often startling. For example, many discarnate entities assert that far from being frozen in a linear sequence of time, our past lives are actually occurring simultaneously, and it is only our belief that the past is frozen and unalterable that keeps us from realizing that at an*

unconscious level we are communicating with our
past and future selves all the time.[lxxiii]

This was yet another reference to simultaneous Time which I didn't appreciate on first reading. In addition, this quote describes ongoing communication with these Past and Future lives; a two-way street. Talbot takes this a step further with another reference to the non-linear nature of Time:

> *To emphasize this point, rather than use the term past*
> *lives, James suggests that we employ the term adjacent*
> *lives, for, as he explains, the life that is affecting us the*
> *most at any given moment may not be our most recent*
> *incarnation but can be any one of our multitude of*
> *existences, no matter how seemingly remote, in what*
> *we currently perceive as space and time.*[lxxiv]

The best example of how Adjacent lives interact comes from an image Talbot presents from "James," which continues to expand awareness with continued application: the "Pocketful of Coins":

> *Indeed, he (James) asserts that instead of being laid*
> *out in a neat line, our various incarnations are actu-*
> *ally part of a much more active and unstable arrange-*
> *ment. As he (James) explains, "the easiest analogy*
> *is to imagine a roll of pennies, each with a different*
> *consecutive date from 1800 to 1985, all stacked in*
> *chronological order. Some exuberant, youthful hand*
> *knocks over the stack, and all the coins roll and scat-*
> *ter, coming to rest everywhere—atop each other, next*
> *to one another, heads up or down. 1896 may be right*
> *next to 1930. 1815 may lie atop 1964. 1918 may have*
> *rolled off under the bureau, and never be heard from*
> *again. And so it is with our lives, your incarnations.*
> *The greater being that is your Oversoul is constantly*
> *rattling the spare change in its pockets, and so your*

'present' life is constantly coming in contact with other past and future lives that may be quite distant in terms of chronological time, but extraordinarily intimate in terms of their psychological presence."[lxxv]

According to James it is when two of these coins, or past lives, stick together that problems surface such as those that come to the fore during a past life regression. By realizing that we can "berth" next to any past or adjacent life that we choose, we can access positive past life influences and experiences.[lxxvi]

Bravo! I love the image of how those "echoes" from our Adjacent lives could be caused by some "greater being…rattling the spare change in its pockets." I'm still amazed that the best description of our Other lives interacting with our Present life came through a "discarnate entity." This is the work I do with my Past Life Journeying process: set an intention to "berth" next to any other life to "access positive Past-life influences or experiences," or to notice when an Adjacent life has "berthed" next to ours, bringing energies and emotions from a non-obvious source.

Since I am stressing that discernment requires that we insist on knowing who these "discarnate entities" are, I was glad that Talbot shared this view:

In subsequent trance sessions James has revealed that, like many such alleged discarnate entities, he is a plurality of beings, a gestalt of consciousness that now inhibits a non-physical level of reality that is no longer subject to the bounds of time. Although it is difficult for those of us who are still constrained by time to imagine what timelessness would be like, James alleges that because he is through with incarnating in a linear timeframe, he can actually be viewed as Tam Mossman's future self.[lxxvii]

I had read *Your Past Lives* multiple times but somehow missed that reference to Mossman's Future self! Talbot's discernment is in evidence when he affirms something that hasn't been given enough attention: the effect of what I call the human channel's "filter" and how it can limit the information coming through from the non-physical:

> *It should be stated that discarnate entities do not always agree with one another in their assessments of the reincarnation process. Similarly, many such entities also caution that their communications are more or less restricted by the vocabulary and understanding of the human channels.*[lxxviii]

I understand the possibility that this can occur in Past Life Journeying, especially when we are new to this process. Confidence comes with experience.

Since reading Talbot's and Mossman's work, I now refer to Past and Future lives as "Adjacent" lives and urge you to think of them from this perspective. I know the standard search engine term for my work is "Past life regression" (even though I don't do regressions), but I found using "Other" or "Adjacent" lives creates a subtle shift in perception to express the range of timelines I encounter, both with clients and in my personal sessions. Merely switching from "Past" to "Other" or "Adjacent" requires stretching the conventional framework…the first step to coloring outside the lines. I use the terms Past/Other/Adjacent interchangeably depending on the context but advise that you try working them into your thought process on "Past" lives. See if it helps you shift to a more nuanced concept of Time.

I credit the discarnate entity known as "James" for this breakthrough concept and acknowledge my indebtedness to Talbot for pushing me past my preconceptions. Michael Talbot dropped his physical form a year after the 1991 publication of *The Holographic Universe*, at age 38, leaving behind four non-fiction books, two novels, and a very grateful "Adjacent" lives researcher in Asheville, NC.

Next: time loops and information from a Future source.

> *The basic picture that Seth, James, and many other discarnate entities offer…is that…ultimately we are beings without borders, complex and constantly fluctuating systems of impulses, self-awareness, and propensities, which are in turn part of a dauntingly vast spiritual ecology, a complex and infinitely interpenetrating ocean of consciousness, that permeates not only all corners of our own universe, but numerous other universes and timeless realms as well.*
>
> Michael Talbot, *Your Past Lives*[lxxix]

ERIC WARGO ON TIME LOOPS AND THE BLOCK UNIVERSE THEORY

> *The thrust of much Futurism since the 1950s has been toward space exploration, the prospect of colonizing Mars, and exploiting the solar system's resources. But I think the real final frontier for our species (and any intelligent, technological civilization) is going to be Time. Our destiny, if we do not destroy ourselves, is to become timefarers and something like history gardeners, sowing seeds in the past for a better tomorrow.*
>
> Eric Wargo, The Nightshirt.com, "Time Portals, Time Drones, and Timeships"[lxxx]

$\mathbf{I}$f you stayed with me this far, welcome fellow Timefarers and "history gardeners"! In my search for a better understanding and some scientific background, I was introduced to a 2018 book by Eric Wargo called *Time Loops: Precognition, Retrocausation, and the Unconscious*. Wargo has a doctorate in anthropology and this was, amazingly, his first book, although he blogs extensively at the Nightshirt.com, where I found the excerpt above. *Time Loops* delivered another piece of the Time puzzle for me, which makes it worth unpacking his key concepts. This is his basic idea:

> *Information from our future somehow seems able to exert an influence over our behavior...That it so often seems to operate outside of conscious awareness*

*suggests that precognition may be a very primitive,
basic guidance system.*[lxxxi]

Wargo sees this idea—that "future events exert an influence over present behavior"—in everything from Freudian theory of the unconscious mind to neuroses and magic, from clairvoyance, telepathy, and the creative process to the double slit experiment that upended Newtonian physics. Wargo also sees that *every* incident of extra sensory perception (ESP) is actually information from the Future looping back to the Present.

The book's subtitle, *Precognition, Retrocausation, and the Unconscious* helps set the stage further. According to him, precognition is *the accessing of knowledge a person will acquire in his or her own future, often directly related to some rewarding or troubling learning experience ahead. Precognition is about our personal experiences, not about other people's experiences or events in objective reality.*[lxxxii] This focus on *personal* experience is central to Wargo's theory about Time Loops.

Time Loops are *baffling, causally circular situations in which a precognitive experience (future knowledge) partly contributes to the fulfillment of the recognized event.*[lxxxiii] To unpack that further: an event in the Future creates or adds to an event in the Present, creating a circular pattern between Future and Present. I was seeing this in my TimeLine Journeying sessions (as we'll see when I introduce you to "George," my 29th century Future life). It took reading *Time Loops* to recognize how this dynamic operates behind the scenes, which is why I included this material.

"Retrocausation" is reversed causality, the opposite of Newtonian physics' "every action has an equal and opposite reaction." Wargo proposes that Time is a continuum comprised of Past, Present, and Future, in which the Future can—and does—directly influence the Present to provide awareness of a Future experience-to-come; the reaction can seem to precede the action. This aligns with Goldberg's concept that the cause of an event could be in the Future.

Got all that? It took me a while, and I had to do some reframing to comprehend how his ideas fit into my TimeLine Journeying. *Time Loops* provides an excellent scientific background to Time (which he always spells with a capital "T"), and his research includes reams of historical data and events that strongly supports the idea that Time does not work the way we are led to believe.

The most fascinating historical precedent for his theory is the case of Morgan Robertson, who in 1898 authored a novel titled *Futility, or the Wreck of the Titan.* As Wargo recounts:

> Futility *tells the story of Lieutenant John Rowland, a once-promising naval officer who has fallen into disgrace because of his drinking and is now working as a common sailor on the new, massive, "indestructible" ocean liner,* Titan. Titan *is making her third round-trip voyage across the Atlantic, from New York to Liverpool...*
>
> Titan, *moving at an unsafe 25 knots through thick fog, is unable to avoid a collision with a smaller ship, which it cuts in two, killing all the smaller vessel's passengers...(Then) an iceberg looms out of the fog ahead and slices into the* Titan's *starboard side, causing it to fall over on its side and drown most of the passengers.*[lxxxiv]

Other writers have seen Robertson's book as prophetic for his capture of many details about the 1912 sinking of the *Titanic*, including its almost-identical name, size, speed, "unsinkable" construction, destination, and lack of lifeboats for the number of passengers.

Robertson himself disavowed any clairvoyant powers, stating "No, I know what I'm writing about, that's all." But Wargo's *Time Loops* model demands precognition be *about our personal experiences, not about other people's experiences or events in objective reality.* In other words, it is

Robertson's response to the disaster that looped back to his writing of the book. Wargo writes:

> (H)e seems to have thought that drink was a necessary tool to get in touch with his muse. He felt unable to write when his muse was not available, which probably drove him to drink more to get it back, in a kind of vicious cycle. Robertson regarded himself, and was regarded by his many friends, as a kind of tragic psychic, constantly frustrated that his prophetic gift could not somehow redeem him. Very sadly, alcohol addiction left Robertson, in his early fifties, a destitute and forgotten failure in his own eyes. He died three years after the Titanic disaster, in 1915, at age 54, in an Atlantic City, New Jersey, hotel room.[lxxxv]

In Wargo's *Time Loops* model, this book I am writing is an example of precognition, where *future events exert an influence over present behavior*[lxxxvi]:

> ...the very act of recording ideas and inspirations may induce an "altered state" conducive to channeling information from a writer's future. It is like attaching a printer directly to the phenomenon of interest... Is "inspiration"—which originally meant possession by a divine spirit—simply a psychologically neutral term for drawing precognitively or presentimentally on a writer's own future?[lxxxvii]

That I may be drawing on my Future to write this book today is a unique take on the creative process! But here is where my experiences diverge from *Time Loops* and involves what is known in physics as the "Block Universe."

Based on the 1908 work of physicist Hermann Minkowski, the Block Universe is a concept in which...*the Past still exists and the Future already* exists and—by implication—nothing is subject to alteration.[lxxxviii] In his Nightshirt blog Wargo cites that in the Block Universe construct *our forays into the Past were already included in our histories*[lxxxix]. The Future—in the case of this book, for example—is complete, set in stone as the "block" image suggests. So, I am simply accessing this knowledge (that I will have in the Future) because *the universe is a fixed block where time only seems to pass.*[xc]

This is a limited version of Simultaneous lives. According to writer Chris Young, *the Block Universe Theory is also known in some scientific circles as Eternalism because it describes how the past, present, and future all co-exist "now."*[xci] In this perspective, which is 100% materialist, Past-Future-Present time co-exist...but nothing can be altered.

Wargo's work is amazing. I highly recommend the book and appreciate its physics-based reappraisal of Time. But my experience differs from his. In my sessions, clients sometimes report that the Other life personality has some psychic awareness of their Past or Future self being present. In other words, their Past- or Future life personality senses the presence of the Other life self who is *running* that event. This becomes more common with experienced Past Life Journeyers as they traverse multiple sessions.

To me, this provides evidence for the reality of Simultaneous lives and, in my humble opinion, refutes any idea of a "fixed" Block Universe where nothing can be altered. Otherwise the presence of this Past or Future self would have had to be, as Wargo believes, *already included in our histories.* But I applaud Wargo for introducing this concept of Time Loops into the discussion around Time, now always referenced with a capital "T."

So, *what if...*

> ...events from our Adjacent lives loop back into our Present incarnation? What if this loop occurs in both directions—energies from either Past or Future lives move into the Present, *or* from our Present life into Past *and* Future lives? (Recall how James' metaphor of

the pocketful of coins gave an example of how these Adjacent lives intersect with our Present life.)

I'll leave you with this quote from an interview Wargo did with Greg Bishop on his *Radio Misterioso* podcast:

> *Just to realize that your mind is transcending the Present moment, and that even if you consciously feel like you're here in your body, sitting at your desk, whatever you're doing in that moment…your mind is transcending that profoundly. And, possibly, even that it's…extending across your whole life. That's the argument I'm trying to make because there are experiences—recorded experiences—that do suggest our behavior, our thoughts right now in the Present moment, could be shaped by events that will happen decades from now.*[xcii]

Yes, and as suggested by Bruce Goldberg, our thoughts and behaviors today could be *shaping* events that happened lifetimes ago. And, as "James" suggested, our thoughts and behavior in the Present moment could be shaped by coming into contact with our Past and Future Adjacent lives when the Oversoul "rattles the coins in its pocket."

Stay tuned and keep asking questions.

My practice of Past Life Journeying is based on freeing up energy blocked by Past and Future "unfinished business," because with this new awareness of Time, the cause of a Present life issue can be embedded in the Past *or* the Future. Tearing up contracts, along with applying gratitude and forgiveness, leads to healing energy, which affects all our lives—Past, Present, and Future. Then, by asking, "What do I need to see next?" we set our intention for our higher self to guide us to the Adjacent life that we most need to see at the time of our journey.

This is how I approach my own work with Past Life Journeying. You can have a mind-blowing, consciousness-expanding experience without drugs (or technology). When we open our consciousness to the process of Past Life Journeying, we can begin to appreciate how information and experiences from all our lives—Past, Present, and Future—"loop" into our Present life because they are occurring *simultaneously*. And, since all our lives are occurring simultaneously, our Present life is "looping" into our Past and Future Adjacent lives.

I've had personal understanding with this "looping" when I experience abilities and talents in my Adjacent lives that I am still striving to cultivate in my Current life. In exploring the Bedouin Mailman's clarity of mind, Maleek's spiritual advancement, and my Future personality "George" with the application of telepathy in his working life, I've come to understand how their lives loop back into mine, especially in the way the mastery of their skills intersects with my Present-day aspirations (and frustrations) around acquiring those same skills. Additional Past Life Journeying sessions provided a subtle awareness of those Adjacent lives being "nourished and fertilized" by my Present-day aspirations (more on that in Book 2), further supporting the reality that all our lives are occurring simultaneously.

With infinite love and gratitude to Eric Wargo for drawing my attention to this Looping process, and Bruce Goldberg, Michael Talbot, and "James" for my new and ever-expanding awareness of Time. Next, I'll introduce you to "George," my Future life personality from the 29th century.

GEORGE—MY 29TH CENTURY FUTURE LIFE

It all hinges on time. We cannot become more than we have time to become. We cannot play a greater part than we have time to learn. Reincarnation gives us reason to ask larger questions about what we are and what our place in the scheme of things is. It also gives us cause to expect larger answers to these questions. When we begin to glimpse our true longevity, when we begin to appreciate the true scope of our lives, we can no longer see ourselves as simply the citizens of one country or one century. We must instead come to see ourselves as time travelers with unrestricted passports.

Christopher Bache, *Lifecycles: Reincarnation and the Web of Life*[xciii]

In April 2020 Dr. Bruce Goldberg gave an online webinar titled "Past Life Regression/Progression and Time Travel" (the best $33 I ever spent!). This was the first opportunity I had to experience his process since hearing him speak a few weeks earlier. After a lecture updating us on his journey, Dr. Goldberg conducted an online group hypnosis session, combining a Past life regression with a Future life progression.

To my complete surprise, I discovered a Future incarnation of mine from the 29th century. Why was I so surprised? (Notice I said "surprised," not "doubtful.") Because I've been one of many people who declared, "This is my last life. Let me finish my work here and go 'home.' I am *not* coming back to this planet." I'd heard this sentiment from many clients even before the Covid lockdown of 2020, which added to their stress in the modern era. Since "George" is my next life in linear time, I apparently *do* remain outside of a physical incarnation for close to 800 years before returning. Maybe the prospect of living in a domed house in the desert and working with extraterrestrials is too enticing? More likely there are greater forces at work.

I have explored this Future life extensively, *running* over two dozen sessions to date and accumulating 40+ hours of recordings—all transcribed for easier access. This is more than any of my Other/Adjacent lives, in part because the life is so fascinating and because it simply required multiple journeys to grasp the details of what I call the "science fiction reality" of life on Earth 800 years in the future. Fortunately, I followed my own advice and took notes immediately after Dr. Goldberg's session:

Bruce Goldberg Webinar Notes

- Forward far into the future, maybe 2820?

- Male, lives in a domed house in the desert

- Everything is futuristic in the home environment, so I nicknamed him "George" after the dad in the 1960's cartoon *The Jetsons*

- I work at The Center, the Unified Space-something center, where we interface with multiple alien races, like a galactic United Nations

- I am an ambassador of sorts; my superpower is "no fear"

- No matter what I am presented with, I remain neutral, whether it's beautiful or ugly, humanoid or non-humanoid in form

- I have a telepathic connection with these other races, receiving concepts, sometimes pictures, no need for translators, just one-on-one communication

- Previously, diplomats wouldn't come back because they would be absorbed into the higher consciousnesses of those whom they encountered, like overwhelmed early LSD trippers who didn't come back from their experiences. (My emphasis on "coming all the way back" may be an "echo" or loop from George's life into my Present life)

Here are some tantalizing details from the first follow-up session I did on my own:

- The house in the desert is inside a dome; instead of a half-acre lot, it's a half-acre dome

- Because it is inside a dome, there is no need for a solid roof, so I have one that is retractable—I have this beautiful image of my wife and I lying in bed underneath a "roof" of desert stars at night

- I work for what we call "The Program," a scientific research operation of cosmic proportions that was in place long before I was born

- In trying to grasp the details of George's job, I jokingly refer to him as "part-ambassador, part-concierge, with a bit of 'doorman at the bar in *Star Wars*' thrown in"

- I interface with multiple alien species; some of these alien ambassadors become my "regular" clients

- In the same way that our local Asheville airport is regional compared to, say, the international status of Charlotte's airport, I work in the equivalent of an "international" spaceport

It's amazing how this Future life "loops" backwards into my Present life. I am drawn to the desert, visiting as often as possible, especially the area east of Las Vegas where I believe George lives and works in that Future timeline. I also attend UFO conferences and stay up on the latest news and events in this field, all of which is to be expected if George's life is Adjacent to mine, and maybe even occurring simultaneously.

You might begin to see how this Future Life Journey took hold of my attention, to the extent that I have explored George's life in over two dozen sessions. There is enough material for a whole other book (hint!), especially with the role that one of my "regular" alien ambassadors plays in my Future Timeline.

There's so much more to explore here:

- George's devotion to this demanding and dangerous job
- Its effect on his relationship with his partner and family
- The intricacies of the technologies used at The Center
- George's family and community connections to The Program
- His co-workers and the higher-ups in the Program
- George's early years and relationships as he devoted himself to the Program
- George's awareness of the history of The Program, and the possibility that it is already in place in my current 21st century Timeline
- The conditions of our planet in 2820, and George's awareness of how the planet has been changed between the 21st century and his Timeline
- How extraterrestrial contact—and the determination to have it—affects society and technology in that era

Past Life Journeying applies the Awareness Technique supplemented with a more heart-based approach—*plus* this new understanding of Time, which encompasses Adjacent lives and the concept of Simultaneous Time.

TimeLine Journeying applies the methods described in this book to explore Future Lives. We are now able to survey the TimeLine of *all* of our lives, stretching from Past to Present to Future lives and beyond. How *far* beyond is still being determined with every session.

Stay tuned for more from George and his/my/our 29th century escapades.

PART 4:
PAST LIFE
JOURNEYING
IN ACTION

*In which Past Life Journeying becomes
my personal spiritual practice.*

> *Most past-life professionals agree and point out that past-
> life therapy is only for people who have a powerful urge to
> grow and stretch beyond the boundaries of their present psy-
> chological, emotional, and spiritual selves, and also have the
> courage to look at themselves honestly and recognize that
> such changes may involve many levels of awareness, behav-
> ior, and patterns of social and personal interaction. Above
> all, a willingness for honest self-understanding is essential.*

Michael Talbot, *Your Past Lives: a Reincarnation Handbook*[xciv]

"I THINK I'M JUST MAKING THIS UP"

To suspend disbelief during a past life regression, simply give yourself permission to experience whatever thoughts, visions, experiences, or ideas come your way, without judgment or criticism. Once you let in all the information that wants to come your way, you can sift through it to hone the accuracy... When we don't allow ourselves to believe in past lives long enough to allow the flow of memories, we will not be able to receive the valuable insights and lessons awaiting us.

Mary Lee Labay, *Exploring Past Lives*[xcv]

Uncertainty is a key issue that needs to be addressed when *running* a Past Life session. The best response is to remember Gail Gulick's Rule #1: *Trust the first image.* Put into practice, this means going along with whatever you see, whether it emerges from outside your expectations, is just too weird, is too close to your Present life, or reflects something you saw in a movie or TV show or read in a book. (And don't ignore the possibility of a Time Loop...being drawn to that book or movie around the same time of your session. Remember the preparation starts when you schedule your session, signaling your intent to undertake the process.)

One session that could have been derailed by doubt was one of my own. I was *running* a session around an emotional issue and the first image I saw when looking down at my feet was a pair of sneakers I recognized from my childhood. Now, I know all of my 20th century lives; I know I couldn't have been wearing that kind of footwear. But I trusted the image and continued exploring the "costume" I was wearing. To my complete surprise, I realized I was *running* an episode from earlier in my Present life, the only time this has ever happened. I *ran* myself as a five-year-old in distress upon hearing that his best friend was moving.

This surprising experience gave me the answer, the message of wisdom I was seeking. And because I trusted that first image, I was able to release some unfinished business, applying gratitude and forgiveness to myself and the adults involved.

Another source of uncertainty is what I call "immersive experience vs. scientific dogma." An article from the August 2021 *National Geographic* magazine inspired a lesson in guiding clients in their Past- and Future life journeys. The article's title (which is now behind a paywall) says it all: "Ancient Rome's Fight Club." In the article, new discoveries once again prodded modern science to reframe long-held beliefs…in this case, beliefs around the ancient Roman gladiators. A new theory, based on the research of Brice Lopez, is this: *a few gladiators were criminals or prisoners of war condemned to combat, but most were professional fighters.*[xcvi]

This new theory points to gladiators as a warrior class, basically professional, highly skilled athletes who thrilled audiences in enormous arenas. Brice Lopez doesn't make the comparison to pro wrestling; that's my attempt to compare it to a modern-day model. But he does postulate the equivalent of fighters "tapping out" instead of fighting to the death.

> *His conclusion: gladiators weren't trying to kill each other; they were trying to keep each other alive. They spent years training in order to stage showy fights, most of which did not end in death. "It's a real competition, but not a real fight," says Lopez, who now runs a gladiator research and reenactment troupe called ACTA. "There's no choreography, but there is good*

intent—you're not my adversary; you're my partner. Together we have to make the best show possible.[xcvii]

It's the background of this that excites me. Plus, my "Spidey Sense" was activated when I read about a man whose Present-day job is running a gladiator reenactment troupe. I can almost *see* his Past life as a gladiator just below the surface of his conscious mind, with insider knowledge of that profession not available in history books.

If a client were accessing a Past life as a gladiator, feeling the "costume" of armor and the thrill of combat, their conscious mind might interrupt their process as, "Wait, I'm fighting with what's basically a chef's knife while wearing as much armor as a Roman soldier? And I've fought my opponent many times before? This can't be right. *I must be making this up.*"

Another—and much stranger—series of incidents were reported in an article on the AcuWeather.com website: "40-foot wave of molasses razed Boston community more than a century ago." This article describes a 1919 catastrophe that occurred when a 2.3-million-gallon tank of molasses burst and destroyed the town, causing eleven deaths. From the article:

> *Most of the time, the word "flood" means a torrent of water rushing into a populated area, destroying property and taking lives. It might come from a river, a lake, runoff from heavy rainfall or a surge from an ocean, but it's water all the same.*
>
> *However, floods with no water at all do happen, and they have devastating impacts, not only economically but on the environment. Of the earliest in recorded history two stand out: the London beer flood in 1814, and the Dublin whiskey fire in 1875.*[xcviii]

Imagine the Past life explorer whose senses are telling him that either he or his loved ones are dead or dying from a flood...but in a flood that isn't water. It's either thick and gooey, or smells like beer or whiskey. It would be all too easy to think, "*I must be making this up.*"

I don't pursue this work for the purpose of gathering historical data, but knowing that uncanny and anomalous tragedies like these *do* occur means we may have them in our Soul's record. Especially if that death was traumatic and echoes into our Present life with health, addiction, or relationship issues, we have to be willing to look beyond the "expected" to the challenging and abnormal. We need to trust the images or information that come to us in a Past life session.

A pattern emerging in recent sessions involves challenging commonly held beliefs about what modern science has decreed to be fact. Past Life Journeying is about having "boots on the ground" and experiencing the inner world of people living their daily lives in circumstances that might be difficult for our 21st-century selves to grasp. It requires surrendering to the process in order to access the inner state of the Adjacent- or Other life personality.

I don't devote much research to finding historical confirmation of Past life events, so I'm grateful when discoveries such as those of Brice Lopez confirm my belief that it *is* possible to get better data from Past Life Journeys than from historical texts, especially when those historical proclamations are re-written on a regular basis. More importantly, there is a skill set developed in trusting our impressions and following through, even though our conscious mind may push back when it doesn't fit an accepted scientific paradigm. This is a prerequisite for Future Life Journeying, which starts at the boundaries of believability. It takes practice and experience to accept what seems like a science fiction reality, which is why I won't guide a Future Life Journey until someone has navigated multiple Past- and Between life sessions.

My own research into paranormal phenomena opened me to a greater understanding of this planet's history and a possible Timeline that extends into previous advanced human civilizations on Earth whose artifacts are assumed to be from off-planet. Hence, the "Ancient Aliens" theory.

In many of the Past life sessions that take place in what we now know as Egypt, clients describe technologies and abilities that surpass what we possess in the 21st century. But there are "alternative" archeologists whose research describes a much greater Timeline than what is accepted and taught. In fact, at the UFO conference I attended in 2020, the first two presentations featured evidence from ancient sites of possible advanced building technologies along with remains that featured elongated skulls. Although these findings were evidence-based and mind-blowing, they were dismissed by the scientific establishment, and the researchers dealt with a fallout of ridicule in their careers.

In a previous example from my own personal sessions, I related a Past life as Maleek, a monk living and working in a mountain retreat where psychic and healing abilities surpass those of modern science. Traditional sources would place this occurring in Tibet, which has a long history of spiritual teachers living in caves high up in the Himalayas. But when I asked, "Where on the planet is this occurring?" my guidance revealed this was taking place in Persia (where modern-day Iran is located.) Also recall that Maleek's life occurred so far in the Past that the mountain where his monastery was located doesn't even exist anymore. Trusting the information I received allowed me to continue exploring rather than attempt to fit this into the traditional setting of Tibet and its Buddhist culture.

Experience has shown that it doesn't have to be uncanny or anomalous information that activates the "*I must be making this up!*" syndrome. Here is an example of my own session where I encountered a personality uncomfortably close to my own: a musician having difficulty handling success, or rather a lack of success. Here are my notes on the musician I called "Johann":

- Black shoes with a buckle, white stockings to the knee, pants of a velour/corduroy-type material that come down to below and button behind the knee, puffy white shirt, silk scarf around the neck which ties in front

- Playing an instrument more like a harpsichord with two keyboards; it's effortless, like breathing

- Aware of the room I'm in, a ballroom in an opulent house with a winding staircase in the entry hall where I am introduced to the attendees, all very wealthy

- But I'm not playing concert halls, this is a "country home circuit" that top level/established musicians would never play; I know I am three or four levels down from the "big-city concert circuit" in spite of possessing great talent

- I drink a lot and have many affairs which get me in trouble, along with (probably) a bad reputation adding to my diminished status

- Interesting detail: very aware of the air in the space, stuffy from hundreds of candles lighting the room, but windows are closed so candles don't blow out. (I was always sensitive to the air in the clubs where I played as a drummer in this life. I always had a fan by my side to provide air flow, since these were days when smoking was still allowed in bars)

- Life didn't end well: on the run from sleeping with the daughter of a powerful man, I was banished from even the country home circuit, and ended my life teaching music in a small town, dying alone

This life, one of the first lives I *ran* back in the 1980s, definitely evoked a powerful "*I must be making this up*" energy. But it wasn't because it was a hard-to-believe culture or setting; it was because it tracked *too* closely with my Present life, a sentiment I have heard from multiple clients. In this life I *always* thought I should be playing concert stages instead of bars, and all of my visualizations were of much bigger successes. I *absolutely* knew what Johann was feeling, playing to the wealthy and powerful, knowing I was merely after-dinner entertainment. This "echoed" into my Present life, especially at the end of my career when the better-paying gigs were in restaurants, playing quietly to not disturb dinner table conversations. I must have taken some lessons from Johann, as alcohol was never a part of my life. I never drank on the job.

This example taught me that when a Past life personality feels *too* much like our Present life, it can be just as difficult to accept as a life where circumstances are completely different from our current situation. A significant step forward in progress is when we start trusting our higher consciousness to show us the life we most need to see at the time of the session. This is what it means to "welcome the guidance I most need at this time," from the intention-setting exercise in my Solo Session Process (which I'll describe shortly).

The other side of this "*I must be making this up*" phenomena is the dreaded "Cleopatra" syndrome. The most common dismissal of Past lives work by the media is, "Why are there so many Cleopatras out there?" This is in reference to *too* many people who claim to be a famous historical figure such as Cleopatra or Julius Caesar. When digging beneath the surface, I usually find those people were *told* they were that famous or historical figure by a psychic or (in my humble opinion) a less-than-scrupulous practitioner.

But I will allow that, especially in the early stages of this work, our deeper consciousness may sometimes offer up an image of a historical figure or famous celebrity. My advice is to open yourself to the possibility that you were someone *close* to a famous figure, and your proximity may grant you "insider information" that can be misconstrued. Deeper digging in a follow-up session should provide definitive evidence one way or the other. (And if it *is* true, imagine the database of experience you can draw into your Present life!)

Michael Talbot proposes a way to confront this head-on if it arises in a Past lives session:

(I)f you see an image of Marilyn Monroe, do not automatically assume that you have some sort of past-life association with Marilyn Monroe. Instead, ask yourself what Marilyn Monroe represents to you on an archetypal or symbolic level, and see if that image helps you unravel the message your unconscious is giving you.

- Michael Talbot, *Your Past Lives*[xcix]

But this still takes "information" from these historical sources, which is different from inhabiting that personality's Past life physical body. In my Past Life Journeying process, the intent is seeing through the eyes, hearing through the ears, and feeling what that personality was going through. If someone claims to have been Cleopatra, I am driven to ask:

- What was her inner life like?

- How comfortable was she in her ruling position?

- Did she really love Antony and what was their relationship like?

- What was her emotional state in the days leading up to her death?

- And lastly, what is the message from this lifetime as Cleopatra for your Present life?

- Are any events, relationships, or emotions "echoing" into your Present life?

Without asking and receiving an answer to these questions, it's just like reading from a book. Wisdom derived from even the greatest of history books cannot compete with the life lessons from a deep Past Life Journey.

PAST LIFE JOURNEYING AS A SPIRITUAL PRACTICE

It does no harm to the mystery to know a little about it.

Richard Feynman, *The Feynman Lectures on Physics*, Vol. 1ᶜ

W hy pursue Past Life Journeying? Writing this book has nudged me to come up with new answers to this question…answers that were much more subtle than I expected. The Covid lockdown and cancellation of public events which started in the spring of 2020 gifted me the opportunity to do many more personal journeys than client sessions. I guided myself through the technique described in this book, and credit it in developing my enhanced appreciation for the power of this work.

But my extended deep dive into my Past lives made me realize that it had also become my personal spiritual practice. Past Life Journeying is my starting place when dealing with personal matters—career dead ends, healing crises, relationship (or lack thereof) issues, and even an expanded perspective toward world events. In multiple timelines, and from multiple perspectives, I can call on experiences from all sides of the economic and social spectrum in navigating pandemics, financial meltdowns, and social/political upheavals.

However, I understand more than ever that this deeper-level work might be a path followed by very few. If I haven't pointed this out yet: ouch! Your higher consciousness doesn't pull punches. When you ask to see the root cause of an issue, be prepared to get spiritually spanked. Past Life Journeying is not for everybody; you have to be willing to let go, if only for an hour or two, of your attachment to the current personality, physical form, and culture in which you've been marinating your entire life. And then…use that Adjacent path as a starting point for a new awareness of your larger self, beginning with the similarities and differences between your Present, Past, and Future "selves."

You'll find it's sometimes in the similarities of these lives, more than in the differences, that we recognize our patterns. We can use them to decide whether we're on a path we love or how, when, and where we lost our way. We can see the choices we made in Other lives and contrast them to our Present choices. When doing this deep digging in a session with a client, I always let them know their discoveries are something they don't need to tell me or say aloud; their privacy is affirmed.

Suggestions for Your Personal Past Life Journeys

- Ask to see your most positive/happiest life. How you define happiness is your own choice, whether that means accomplishing life goals, relationship "success," or any criteria such as health, abundance, etc.

- Explore the highest and best experience of your favorite criteria for success in life: "Health, Wealth, Wisdom, and Peace" are mine. (This can be four separate journeys, although more than one may be found in a single life.)

- If you have a personal connection to a spiritual figure or guru, ask to see the life where you may have personally interacted with them or their followers. This could be Jesus, the Buddha, Mohammed, any other religious leader, a guru such as Paramahansa Yogananda, an ancient Egyptian or other god or goddess to which you're attracted.

- If you don't have a specific person in mind, ask to see the life where you interacted with the most spiritually advanced person from all your lives.

- If you consider wealth to be important to your journey in this lifetime, ask to see the wealthiest, most abundant life you've lived. It's important to explore how that achievement of wealth influenced your life and your personal goals. Did it smooth the path to inner peace or deflect you into mindless extravagance? Remember, there is no blame; this information does not have to be shared with anyone and can be a powerful incentive for journaling.

- Many clients want to know more about their life's purpose. Ask to see the plans you made for your Current life and who agreed to work with you on those plans.

- To explore purpose further, ask to see your First life in a human body, along with your decision to incarnate in what Dolores Cannon calls "The Earth School." This was a fascinating suggestion from William J. Baldwin. I've been working on this myself, and it's taken ongoing, multiple sessions to unpack all the details.

- Explore your Present life's work by asking to see the Adjacent lives where you were also involved in this activity. This is something I am exploring in my Timeline Journeying process, where we construct the TimeLine of a career or passion project.

- If you have an interest in the increasingly popular CE-5 protocol for interacting with extraterrestrials, consider that the activities into which you are drawn in this life may be an "echo," or loop, from our involvement in a similar activity in an Other or Adjacent lives—Past, Present, or Future. Ask to see Other lives where you had these interactions. I have personally done this with multiple clients and the results have been more spiritually uplifting than science fiction. My only caveat: just because these "visitors" appear to have superior technology, don't assume this is an indication of spiritual superiority. *Discernment is always the most important approach.*

Next, I'll show you how I conduct my personal sessions, step-by-step.

INSTRUCTIONS FOR GUIDING
A PAST LIFE JOURNEY

The following is based on the original instructions first published and distributed by William and Diane Swygard in 1970. I have evolved and expanded them based on hundreds of my own sessions, plus group and individual sessions with my clients and the participants in the Past Lives Project. (Since I conduct most of my sessions with the client seated in front of me, these instructions refer to the body in the chair. If lying down or sitting cross legged on the floor, adjust them to suit your position):

> When well-rested and in a quiet place, close your eyes and take a moment to feel the chair supporting you. Because the best inhalation starts with a long exhalation, breathe out all the air in your lungs, hold for a second, and breathe in deeply. Then, breathe out and allow the exhale to be longer than the inhale. This will effectively activate the body's innate relaxation response.
>
> Now, trust that your body knows how to breathe. Trust the chair to hold you up. Put your attention on the bottoms of your feet. Since energy flows where attention goes, you may feel a slight tingling at the bottoms of your feet. Become a few inches taller by allowing your consciousness to stretch a few inches out through the bottom of your feet. Take as long as you need, and tell me as soon as you have done this. Now return to normal height, and tell me as soon as you have done this. Then once again become a few inches taller by allowing your consciousness to stretch through the bottom of your feet. Return to normal height once again.

Now become a whole *foot* taller by allowing your consciousness to stretch through the bottom of your feet. Tell me as soon as you have done this. Then return to normal height. Once again, become a foot taller by stretching through the bottom of your feet. Return to normal height.

Now go to the other end of the body and put your attention on the top of your head. Become a few inches taller by allowing your consciousness to expand outward through the top of your head. Tell me as soon as you have done this. Return to normal height. Then become a *foot* taller by allowing your consciousness to expand through the top of your head. Tell me as soon as you have done this. Then return to normal height.

Now, allow your consciousness to expand in all six directions:

> Down, through the bottom of your feet,
> up, through the top of your head,
> forward, through the front of the body,
> backward, through the back of the body,
> outward, through the left side of the body,
> and outward, through the right side of the body.
> In other words, blow up like a balloon and tell me as
> soon as you have done this.
> Then return to normal size.

Once again, allow your consciousness to blow up like a balloon in all six directions, but *larger* this time: down, up, forward, out the back, to the left, and to the right.

Feel a bubble of energy surrounding your body. Allow this bubble of energy to float up through the ceiling, continuing up through the roof of the building you are in. Stand on the roof of the building you are in and look down at the area in front of the building. Tell me what you see from this vantage point on the roof.

Next, turn your attention to the back of the building and describe what you see from this vantage point on the roof.

Allow your energy bubble to float 500 feet up into the air. Tell me as soon as you are there. Look down and tell me what you see from the vantage point of 500 feet above this building and the neighborhood.

Is it daytime or nighttime?

> If it's daytime: make it nighttime and tell me what you see from the vantage point of 500 feet above your house and neighborhood at night. Then, make it daytime again, and tell me as soon as you have done this. Once again, make it nighttime and tell me as soon as you have done this. Now make it daytime one last time. Make it a bright sunny day and allow yourself to be surrounded with light.

> If it's nighttime: make it daytime and tell me what you see from the vantage point of 500 feet above your house and neighborhood. Then make it nighttime, and tell me as soon as you have done this. Then make it daytime one last time. Make it a bright sunny day and allow yourself to be surrounded with light.

This is the starting point for your Past Life Journey. Set your intention for this session:

> I open myself to a message of wisdom from a Past life
> and welcome the guidance I most need at this time.

Do you agree with this intention? If you do, then allow your energy bubble to float high up above the earth. Imagine being in a cloud surrounded by light. From this vantage point high above the planet, allow your energy bubble to float down to the ground while also going back in time and space. Allow your consciousness to guide you to the location on the planet, and to the lifetime, that your consciousness wants you to experience, in another body, in another place, in another time. Come down firmly but gently and stand on the ground. Tell me as soon as you are there.

Look down at your feet and tell me what—if anything—is covering your feet. (If you aren't the fortunate visual type, *feel* what is covering your feet, or ask, "What is covering my feet?" and let the answer guide you.) Allow your consciousness to see through the eyes, hear through the ears, and feel what your Past life personality is feeling.

Become aware of where you are standing. Are you indoors or out-doors? Describe the surface on which you are standing. Is it daytime or nighttime?

Become aware of what—if anything—is covering the lower part of your body. How much of the lower part of your body is covered. Are there layers? What do the layers consist of? See, feel, or ask about the texture and color of whatever is covering the lower part of your body.

Put your attention on the upper part of your body. What—if any-thing—is covering the upper part of your body? How much of your upper body is covered? Is it long-sleeved or short? Is it open at the neck or is your neck covered? See, feel, or ask about the texture of the material covering the upper part of your body.

Become aware of your hair. Is it long or short, dark or light, curly or straight? What—if anything—is covering the top of your head? Describe it. Become aware of your face. Is there any facial hair, any makeup or markings? Are you wearing any earrings or necklaces? Describe them.

Look down at your hands and tell me: Are these indoor hands or outdoor hands? Are there any rings or bracelets? Do these rings or bracelets have any emotional significance?

Become aware of the personality wearing this "costume." Is this a female or a male personality? What is the age range of this personality? Is this a child, an adolescent, an adult, middle-aged, or an elder?

Expand your awareness to your surroundings. Are there any people or animals with you, or nearby? Are you carrying anything—any bags, tools, or weapons?

You have connected to this Past life personality in their environment. Feel into the energy of this personality and ask yourself: What is my emotional state of mind?

Feel what your Past life personality is experiencing: Ask what activity you are involved in. Very often our consciousness guides us to an event or activity that gives us information about the inner life of this Past life personality.

Go and stand in front of your house, or wherever you live. Describe it with attention. How does this building or location makes you feel? Then move inside and describe what you see. Are there any other people in the house? Describe them. How does the presence of these people make you feel?

Go forward to a significant event in this person's life. Go there, look around, and tell me where you are and what is going on around you. Note any significant personalities involved. What is your reaction to them? Feel whether you are comfortable in their presence. If not, feel into the discomfort. You are becoming more aware of the inner life of this Past life personality.

If one personality emerges as most significant, feel into the energy of this personality. (If you are a visual type, look into their eyes.) Does this personality resonate with anyone you know or have known in your present life? (They may be of a different age, or even of a different sex or role, but how they make you feel may resemble someone you know or knew in your Present life.)

You can stop at any time by putting an energetic bookmark in the scene, with the intention to revisit it in your next session.

A Past life journey isn't complete until you experience the end of this personality's lifetime. Accomplish this by asking to go to the last day of this person's life. Go there, look around, and describe where you are. What is going on around you? Allow yourself to feel what this personality is experiencing. Note any vows, promises to do better next time, and especially anything that feels left unfinished. Sometimes the information from the end of a life provides the most important take-away from an entire session.

Then allow this personality to leave their body, feeling what they feel and how they respond to their detachment from the physical body. (An entire session can be devoted to this Between lives experience.)

To conclude the session, allow your energy bubble to float up, high above this scene. Bring this energy bubble up into the air above your Present-day body. Ask that more information from this lifetime comes to you: internally in the form of dreams, and externally, from books and movies, bumper stickers and billboards, and even in conversations. You have only just begun to integrate this information; the process will continue.

Allow your energy bubble to float down and connect to your body in the chair. Feel the chair holding you up. Feel the clothes on your Present-day body. Feel your feet on the floor. Breathe yourself back into your Present body. Feel the air in the room. Take as long as you need, and when you are ready, open your eyes.

Close by expressing gratitude: Thank you for trusting me with this experience and this information.

Congratulations! Your consciousness has expanded beyond your Present life and your Present personality on the first step of your soul's journey. Through this first Past Life Journey, know that you are more than this soul, in this body, in this time period.

RUNNING TIP: *RUNNING* PAST LIVES BY YOURSELF

A few years ago, while giving a presentation, I described a personal *running* session from a few hours beforehand which was very fresh in my mind:

- I was a ruler in this life—maybe not a king, but a local wannabe-king—and a pompous ass of one, in the middle ages. I pushed my people too far pursuing my own appetites and was no longer providing for them.

- When they overthrew me, I found myself in a stone-walled prison cell awaiting execution. This was a wake-up moment for me; I realized the error of my ways and negotiated to get my wife and daughter out safely.

- In the backstory that revealed itself, I was given a chance to see the local bishop. I told him where my money was hidden and recruited him to act as my go-between to escort my wife and daughter to safety. Once I got word that my family was safe, I surrendered to my fate. When I asked, "What happens next?" I received my answer verbally: "You're going to be beheaded."

(Sigh)…another pompous ass in my past! I was so glad I related this story to the group, as it opened my *running* process to further examination as I tried to describe my experience. Someone noticed that I used the second person: "You're going to be beheaded," not, "I'm going to be beheaded."

Someone else asked if it was a male or female voice that I heard, or if it was my own voice.

What's interesting is I couldn't answer these questions about my process from outside the process. It wasn't until the next day, when re-visiting the experience, that I recognized it wasn't a clear voice I'd heard; it was more of a "verbal prompt." (This was a subtle insight into my process since verbal clues will often lead me to the visual information). And that the voice was male, but not my own. I never would have investigated my own *running* if I hadn't tried explaining it to others. And in trying to explain it, I uncovered aspects of my process that might assist others who are new to Past Life Journeying. Yet another example where a group moves the work forward, and another reason for me to be grateful for everyone's participation.

In describing how I run a Past life myself, I realized that newer participants were surprised I was able to do the work alone, a great example of "learning by teaching." I am drawn to explaining the step-by-step process to make it easier and more accessible. The key was brought to my attention by a quote from *Transformational Life Coaching: A Seminal View*, where author Zen Benefiel describes "talking to yourself out loud." This is not something that people do naturally; our culture doesn't look kindly on people talking to themselves. But it's important to this process.

Swygard's *Awareness Techniques - Book 1* even addresses this in a brief chapter titled "You Can Work 'Multi-Level Awareness' All By Yourself." (Recall that "Multi-level awareness" is how *Book 1* describes *running* Past lives to distinguish it from the processes described in succeeding books.) Swygard recommends that if you don't have someone to *run* you, take the initial exercise, memorize it, and then practice it yourself. Do the first stretching exercise until you are comfortable with it, then go on to the next step. He writes, "Speak out loud and tell yourself to do these things." When you are comfortable with the first stretching exercise, go to the next step.

I hate to admit I missed the fact that the original instructions for *running* solo featured a recommendation to "speak out loud." I had to rediscover it for myself. (New tricks/old dog?) But it was the most significant upgrade in my ability to access Other lives by myself with the added benefit of leaving a data trail in the recording for future reference. Simple and direct.

Zen Benefiel's quote reminded me of the importance of doing this:

> *There is something very important about talking to yourself out loud. You get to listen. When you are inside your head, and the monkey mind is chattering away, there is little to no listening unless you are very practiced at meditation. Most of us aren't.*

> *There is another example that fits. When we engage another for advice, counseling, or therapy, the real insights come from listening to the words that come out of us, not necessarily the reflection of the other listener. We have a tremendous capacity to process and transform accordingly, and although it's nice to have someone to talk to it isn't always necessary.*[ci]

This came easy for me because I always record my sessions, either using the iPhone Voice Record Pro app, or my MacBook using a Snowball USB microphone plugged into Audacity or GarageBand software. This enables me to record my sessions, label them (for reference, this session was labeled "Beheaded Ruler"), and email them to my desktop iMac to store in the cloud. I have always worked entirely within the Apple universe, but I'm sure there are equivalents for Android phones.

The technique of talking aloud takes some getting used to but is worth the effort. It also helps focus on the most important aspect of *running* by oneself: asking good questions. In the beginning, when working in detail mode—seeing through the eyes, listening through the ears, and tuning into that Previous incarnation's bodily sensations and emotions—the basic question for moving forward is, "What happens next?"

This is time-consuming but necessary. It takes time for the Present-day physical body and its waking consciousness to accept the reality of this other physical body that possibly comes with a different sex or race, and usually in a different location and time period. I call it "navigating" the Previous physical incarnation...like the way we learn to adjust when driving a new vehicle. Once we've learned how to "navigate" in a Previous incarnation and become comfortable with asking, "What happens next?" (which takes some time and practice), we can go a step forward in complexity to guiding by giving directions in addition to asking questions.

This next level allows us to leave linear Time behind and move through a life by examining only the events that relate to the question or desire being addressed. Ask, "What is the next significant event in this life?"

Here we address the choice of using first-person versus second-person questions. When *running* someone else, the most direct question is this, "Move forward to the next significant event in this life. Go there, look around, and tell me: where are you and what's going on around you?"

When working by oneself determine—by practice—whether you are more comfortable asking in first person, "Where am *I*?" vs. the external questioner who asks, "Where are *you* and what's going on around *you*?" As I wrote this, I had to stop and think about whether I address myself in the first or second person. When *running* for others, I always use the second person: "Where are you?" but realized that when working solo, I use the first person: "Where am I and what's going on around me?" The goal is connecting to our Past life personality, seeing through the eyes, hearing through the ears, and feeling what that personality is experiencing.

When we are more comfortable and experienced at "navigating" through a life, we can move through what I call the "greatest hits" version of that life. The questions to ask when moving quickly and confidently through the *running* process is, "What do I need to see in relation to my

Present life?" or, "What do I need to see regarding my question (or issue) that prompted this session?"

Another aspect of navigating is the ability to go backwards in linear Time. If we find ourselves in a complicated situation, we can direct ourselves, "Put a bookmark in this scene. Let's go back to the events leading up to this state of affairs." If my first "clue" in this session is an image of a man sitting in a dank prison cell but dressed in Royal finery, I would first describe his costume, then expand my awareness to his surroundings. I would gather this information to help access his obviously distressed state of mind, then "rewind" to examine those events that led to his imprisonment. (That energetic "bookmark" will guide us back to that initial scenario if we choose to revisit it.)

This questioning process is important, whether we are *running* by ourselves or *running* someone else. Being experienced enough to ask the questions that keep the *running* process moving forward allows us to run multiple lives in one session or see multiple lives in response to a question about a specific topic. *But don't move forward unless, and until, you feel your questions are being answered.* Only you can determine this.

The next step is also vital in successfully navigating this process: keep a journal of your sessions. Whether you *run* with someone else or by yourself, always take time to make notes on your experience as soon as possible afterwards, even if it's just noting keywords. As an example of how this process works when put into practice, I wrote an interesting combination of verbal, visual, kinesthetic, and emotional details for the session in question:

> A*#hole ruler, possibly king. Pissed everyone off with
> his appetites, thrown in prison, fancy clothes now
> dirty, stone walls and floor, cut deal with bishop to
> save wife and daughter, beheaded.

Something else I do for my own sessions is to re-listen to the recordings and transcribe them—sometimes just the significant parts. Other sessions are so action-packed with powerful information that I transcribe the entire hour-plus session (more on this later). I tell clients that even the simple act of listening to the session afterwards is like getting a free second session; details that were missed while in the state of retrieving information take on added significance...even more so if time has passed since the session.

I am always glad I've taken the time to do this. There is so much information being accessed in the hour or 90 minutes of the session that some of it might get missed. Plus, more information arises by re-visiting the process when time has passed and things have seeped further into our Present consciousness.

I invite you to contact me for a Past Life Journeying session. When working with an experienced practitioner—like myself—you can benefit from my skill in asking the intuitive questions to guide you on this journey to your eternal self. And now, with technology to see and hear each other online from our own homes, anyone with internet access can advance confidently toward the answers to our deepest questions...and the self-realization that comes with those answers.

How does someone do this Past- and Between lives work by themselves? Maybe the answer is similar to the answer of that old New York City cab driver's joke: "How do you get to Carnegie Hall? Practice, practice, practice."

MY SOLO SESSION PROCESS

Here's how I conduct my solo sessions. Feel free to adjust it to your own best results.

Items needed:

- A quiet room and a rested body. Staying focused was the main stumbling block when I started working alone. I still suffer from "monkey mind"—more like "King Kong mind"—despite maintaining a daily meditation practice. I'll admit using caffeine or herbal stimulants to aid in mental stamina, and I've experimented with various nootropics (basically vitamins for the brain), including nicotine lozenges and the herbal compound called Brain Pep. (But I don't necessarily advocate using any substances.)

- A comfortable chair. I have an old, high-backed chair, the only item left from the house in which I grew up. I prefer to work sitting up. I conduct client sessions with them seated in front of me, in person or on their computer.

- I use eye shades to limit distractions, and find it helps me stay focused in my inner world. This is another takeaway that I have borrowed from my shamanic journeying sessions with Gail Gulick.

- A recording device. I use an app on my iPhone, or a Blue Snowball USB microphone connected to my laptop, either running on GarageBand or Audacity®. This is because I ask my questions and answer them aloud. I find the audio feedback from answering my own questions key to successful work alone. Plus, it gives me a record of the session, which I listen to in the following days. I later transcribe the important sessions (and they're all important at this stage of my work).

In my discipline, I won't *run* a new session until I've either listened to, or transcribed, the previous session. The few times I've whiffed that, I found myself repeating questions and missing details from the last session. I recognize the degree of altered state which I am in during these sessions, and always discover details I've forgotten—or whose importance I've missed—until I hear the playback.

That's it. Externally: just eye shades, a comfortable chair in a quiet room, and a recording device nearby. If you're *running* a follow-up session, read the transcript or your notes from the previous session. (You're taking notes and keeping them in some accessible form, right?) MS Word, Apple Pages, or Google Docs all work well, and I use all three. I suggest setting up a folder for your sessions. Date them to keep them separate and searchable.

Internally, the next step involves setting my intention for this Past life or Future Timeline journey. I cobbled the following statement from various sources over the years and added my own ideas and alterations...so I can't say where this came from except to express gratitude to whomever contributed. Feel free to add your own modifications:

> I open myself to a message of wisdom from a Past life
> and welcome the guidance I most need at this time.

(Sometimes I substitute the word "knowledge" for "guidance" if that is more in line with my intention.) I advocate using a Past life as a starting point for your intention. Later, the intention can be expanded to asking for wisdom from a Past *or* Future life.

If I am working on an "acute" emotional issue, I'll tune into it and follow the emotion into its Other life origin. But most often I use a shortcut version of the Awareness Technique to stretch out of and detach from the physical body, allow my energy body to float up above the body in the chair, through the roof, and above the house and neighborhood. I found I can get out of my body and connect to my energy body in a minute or two when practicing my version of the original instructions for the Awareness Technique—stretching out of top of the head or bottom of the feet, then returning to normal size...but that took a lot of practice. (By the way, practicing this on its own is an excellent exercise in concentration and energetic focus.)

Another tip from my bag of tricks? 90% of the time, my intention is this: "Show me what I need to know at this time." Or, if this is a follow-up on a Previous lifetime: "What is the next thing I need to know about this Other life personality or issue?" This allows higher consciousness to override my ego and always results in a surprising flow of information. In the case of my two dozen-and-counting sessions journeying to the Future life I call George, I've been guided to different parts of his Timeline—from adulthood to student years, work life to home and family life and back again—a through-line that was very cinematic and unpredictable, but always insightful in the way it revealed the inner workings of his/ my personality.

I always close my sessions with an expression of gratitude, plus an acknowledgement that:

> I have only just begun the process of integrating information from this Other life. This integration process will continue until it is complete, and I open myself to input from both internal sources—dreams and realizations—and external sources—books, movies, conversations, billboards, bumper stickers— whatever I need. Thank you for trusting me with this information.

Try it for yourself, work with a friend who can read the instructions, or contact me for a session.

Happy Journeying!

*Your life in retrospect has much more coher-
ence than it does as you're living it.*

John Mack, Harvard psychiatrist*
*This line came from a talk given at the International Conference on Altered
States of Consciousness in Albuquerque, NM in October, 2002. Mack got a
laugh with this line because it referred to the professional character assassina-
tion he endured when he started writing about people who had alien encoun-
ters and "the transformational aspects of extraordinary experiences."

POSTSCRIPT

The material contained in this book provides the basic "starter kit" for a Past Lives Journey based on the very effective method known as "The Awareness Technique" created by William and Diane Swygard. These basic instructions for expanding beyond the Present-life physical body were my introduction to my Past lives.

Later, when exploring the Between lives state, I experienced my first awareness of having left a body behind when that lifetime was completed. I was outside of Time, specifically outside of Linear Time. That glimpse of being outside of Time stayed with me and it was only years later that I encountered the works of Bruce Goldberg and other practitioners who'd already explored this territory.

Equally amazing is how perfectly my pursuit of dozens of personal Past life sessions (along with those of hundreds of sessions with clients) revealed the path to exploring Future Timelines. This led to my discovery of a Future life in the 2800s, followed by journeying through my Timeline as it extended beyond this brief (in cosmic terms) chapter in the Earth School.

I have over a hundred sessions transcribed from this work, which I am now calling *TimeLine Journeying*. I only undertook this advanced work after years of exploring my Past and Between lives. In launching this book into the world and onto the internet, I hope others drawn to this work will discover it and put it to good use. When it answers their first set of questions, I hope they continue working, and find my next book (already in progress) describing my TimeLine Journeying process in action.

In Book 2 I will introduce you to "George's" fantastic world and his life in the 29th century. Those 20+ sessions spent exploring his/my world provide insight into our planet and its challenges in the 21st century. My personal Spirit name, which I mentioned earlier, plays a big part in the events that formed Book 2. In one of my most challenging sessions, I explore the non-physical experience before my next incarnation, which is Between lives and *after* this Present life. It's an intense journey based on my advanced TimeLine Journeying sessions. These are the landscapes available for investigation with the tools in this starter kit you have in your possession.

Until then, "Ask questions, ask questions, ask questions."

PS: You can always ask me some of those questions at TimeLineJourneying@gmail.com.

PPS: Check out my blog at https://PastLivesProject.org/The-Past-Lives-Project-Blog, where I post my ongoing research into Past, Between, and Future lives.

With integrated Love and Gratitude for your bravery in taking this Soul Journey,

Bobby B.

END NOTES

i   Christopher Bache, *Lifecycles: Reincarnation and the Web of Life* (Paragon House, 1994), 114.

ii Paramahansa Yogananda, *The Divine Romance* (University of Michigan, 1986), 55.

iii Ainslie Macleod, "Why Are Past Lives So Awful?," (Past Life Psychic, July 14, 2016), https://ainsliemacleod.com/why-are-past-lives-so-awful/.

iv William Swygard & Associates, *Awareness Techniques - Book 1* (Theatre University, 1970), 20.

v   Michelle Brandt, "Not getting sleepy? Research explains why hypnosis doesn't work for all" (Stanford Medicine, October 2, 2012), https://med.stanford.edu/news/all-news/2012/10/not-getting-sleepy-research-explains-why-hypnosis-doesnt-work-for-all.html.

vi Hans TenDam, *Exploring Reincarnation: The Classic Guide to the Evidence for Past Lives* (Lulu.com, 2012), 13.

vii Andy Tomlinson, *Exploring the Eternal Soul* (From the Heart Press, 2017) eBook, Preface.

viii Source Unknown.

ix Swygard, *Awareness Techniques*, 10.

x   Swygard, *Awareness Techniques*, 4.

xi Helen Hoag, *Technique of Past Lives Recall* (Metaphysical Research, 1969), 9.

xii Swygard, *Awareness Techniques*, 8.

xiii wikiHow.com/Remembering Your Past Lives

xiv Swygard, *Awareness Techniques*, 11.

xv   Oxford Reference, https://www.oxfordreference.com/view/10.1093/oi/authority.20110803100030507

xvi   Swygard, *Awareness Techniques*, 21.

xvii   https://www.hypnoticworld.com/regression-past-lives/christos-technique

xviii   Various, *The Christos Experiment – Introductory Principles-Booklet No. 5* (Open Mind, 1971), 15.

xix   Jaqueline Parkhurst, *Altered States of Consciousness and the Christos Experiment* (Open Mind, 1976), 18.

xx   Dick Sutphen, "Viewing Past Life Workshop – The Ascension Technique Instructions" (Valley of the Sun, 1999), https://www.youtube.com/watch?v=09FhTiYm2r0&list=OLAK5uy_lZlo7JuxfilGjYUuQa5k2zhPb_vGxdR0

xxi   Swygard, *Awareness Techniques*, 7.

xxii   Swygard, *Awareness Techniques*, 7.

xxiii   Dolores Cannon, "The Lost Knowledge" chapter of the *UFO Chronicles* documentary series), 2019.

xxiv   Richard Bandler, *Using Your Brain for a Change*, (Real People Press, 1985), 8.

xxv   Richard Martini, *It's a Wonderful Afterlife*, (eBook, Homina, 2014), Chapter 1.

xxvi   Christopher Bache, *Lifecycles- Reincarnation and the Web of Life* (Pennsylvania State University, 1998), 128.

xxvii Barbara Stone, *Invisible Roots – How Healing Past Life Trauma Can Liberate Your Present* (Hay House, 2008), Foreword XVIII-XIX.

xxviii Christopher Bache, *Lifecycles*, 71.

xxix   Christopher Bache, *Lifecycles*, 120.

xxx   Allen Craig Houston, *Benjamin Franklin and the Politics of Improvement* (Yale University 2008), 70.

xxxi   *Los Angeles Times*, "I once fell for the fantasy of uploading ourselves. It's a destructive vision" (October 10, 2022).

xxxii Morris Netherton, *Strangers in the Land of Confusion*, (e-book, CreateSpace Independent Publishing Platform,

2015), Preface.

xxxiii   https://www.pastlifetherapycenter.com/WhatisPast-LifeTherapy_FAQ.html

xxxiv   Hans TenDam, *Exploring Reincarnation* (Lulu.com, 2012), 162.

xxxv   Roger Woolger, *Other Lives, Other Selves- A Psychotherapist Discovers Past Lives* (Dolphin/Doubleday, 1987), 142.

xxxvi   Woolger, *Other Lives,* 340.

xxxvii   Woolger, *Other Lives,* 218.

xxxviii   Woolger, *Other Lives,* 29.

xxxix   Dick Sutphen, *Past-Life Therapy in Action* (Valley of the Sun, 1983), 101.

xl   Sutphen, *Past-Life Therapy,* 101.

xli   Sutphen, *Past-Life Therapy,* 103.

xlii   *Naugatuck Daily News,* "Walter Winchell In New York," (Naugatuck, Connecticut April 06, 1949), Page 4 Column 5.

xliii   Woolger, *Other Lives,* 322

xliv   Woolger, *Other Lives,* 212.

xlv   "Watch Springsteen on Broadway" (Netflix , 2018).

xlvi   Dolores Cannon, *ETs and Human Evolution,* (Gaia TV interview with Regina Meredith, Season 6), Episode 31.

xlvii   Wailana Kalama, "Hawaii's Trendy Word That's Misunderstood" (https://www.bbc.com/travel/article/20180916-hawaiis-trendy-word-thats-misunderstood) Sept. 17, 2018.

xlviii   Sylvia Browne, *Past Lives, Future Healing,* (eBook, Penguin, 2001), Chapter 1 and *The Other Side and Back* (eBook, Penguin, 2000), Chapter 5.

xlix   Michael Pollan, The New Science of Psychedelics, *The Wall Street Journal,* (May 3, 2018), https://michaelpollan.com/articles-archive/the-new-science-of-psychedelics/

l   Michael Pollan, *How to Change Your Mind* (Penguin Books, 2019), 307.

li   Pollan, *How to Change Your Mind*, 320.

lii   Christopher Bache, *LSD and the Mind of the Universe*, (eBook, Inner Traditions/Bear, 2019), Chapter 1.

liii   Carl Jung, *Memories, Dreams, Reflections* (University of Michigan, 1965), 199.

liv   Mary Lee LaBay, *Past Life Regression: A Guide for Practitioners*, (eBook Trafford, 2004), Chapter 7.

lv   LaBay, *Past Life Regression*, Chapter 7.

lvi   https://quoteinvestigator.com/2014/04/13/open-mind/

lvii   Labay, *Past Life Regression*, Chapter 7.

lviii   Judd Apatow, *Sick in the Head* (Random House, 2016), 42.

lix   Paramahansa Yogananda, *Autobiography of a Yogi* (Self Realization Fellowship,1946), 3.

lx   Bache, *Lifecycles*, 127.

lxi   Bruce Goldberg, *Past Lives, Future Lives Revealed* (Bruce Goldberg, Inc. 2017), 18.

lxii   Goldberg, *Past Lives*, 24.

lxiii   Goldberg, *Past Lives*, 164.

lxiv   Goldberg, *Past Lives*, 136.

lxv   Goldberg, *Past Lives*, 138-139.

lxvi   Michael Talbot, *The Holographic Universe* (HarperPerennial, 1991), 228.

lxvii   Talbot, *Holographic Universe*, 234.

lxviii   Paramahansa Yogananda, *Man's Eternal Quest* (Self Realization Fellowship, 1975), 225.

lxix   Talbot, *Your Past Lives*, 31-32, 34.

lxx   Talbot, *Your Past Lives*, 163.

lxxi   Talbot, *Your Past Lives*: p. 172.

lxxii   Talbot, *Your Past Lives*, 168.

lxxiii   Talbot, *Your Past Lives*, 170.

lxxiv   Talbot, *Your Past Lives*, 170.

lxxv   Tam Mossman, *Answers from a Grander Self* (Tiger Maple Press, 1993), 177.

lxxvi   Talbot, *Your Past Lives*, 170-171.

lxxvii   Talbot, *Your Past Lives*, 168.

lxxviii   Talbot, *Your Past Lives*, 168.

lxxix   Talbot, *Your Past Lives*, 169.

lxxx   Eric Wargo, "Time Portals, Time Drones, and Timeships," *TheNightShirt.com*, (August 22, 2020), http://thenight-shirt.com/?p=4529.

lxxxi   Eric Wargo, *Time Loops: Precognition, Retrocausation, and the Unconscious* (Anomalist, 2018), 11.

lxxxii   Wargo, *Time Loops*, 41.

lxxxiii   Wargo, *Time Loops*, 11.

lxxxiv   Wargo, *Time Loops*, 281.

lxxxv   Wargo, *Time Loops*, 284-285.

lxxxvi   Wargo, *Time Loops*, 5.

lxxxvii   Wargo, *Time Loops*, 86.

lxxxviii   Wargo, *Time Loops*, 308.

lxxxix   Eric Wargo, "Time Portals, Time Drones, and Timeships," *TheNightShirt.com*.

xc   Chung, Philip. "A Debate Over the Physics of Time," *Quanta*, (July 19, 2016), https://www.quantamagazine.org/a-debate-over-the-physics-of-time-20160719/.

xci   Young, Chris. "Block Universe Theory: Is the Passing of Time an Illusion?" *Interesting Engineering*, (Feb. 11, 2020), https://interestingengineering.com/science/block-universe-theory-is-the-passing-of-time-an-illusion.

xcii   Eric Wargo, "Time Loops and Retrocausality," *Radio Misterioso*, (January 15, 2019), http://radiomisterioso.com/2019/01/15/eric-wargo-time-loops-and-retrocausali-ty/.

xciii   Bache, *Lifecycles*, 114.

xciv   Talbot, *Your Past Lives*, 141-142.

xcv   Mary Lee Labay, *Exploring Past Lives*, (Trafford, 2008), 9-10.

xcvi Andrew Curry. "Ancient Rome's Fight Club," *National Geographic Magazine*, August 2021.

xcvii Andrew Curry. "Ancient Rome's Fight Club," Chapter 1.

xcviii Wyatt Loy, "40-foot wave of molasses razed Boston community more than a century ago," *AccuWeather.com*, (July 18, 2022), https://www.accuweather.com/en/weather-news/40-foot-wave-of-molasses-razed-boston-community-more-than-a-century-ago/1210147.

xcix Talbot, *Your Past Lives* (Harmony, 1987) 62.

c Richard Feynman, *The Feynman Lectures on Physics, Vol. 1* (Basic, 2011), Chapter 3, footnote.

ci https://www.facebook.com/profile/697642959/search/?q=talking%20to%20yourself%20out%20loud